Crawley and Dis

in old picture postcards

by
Michael Goldsmith

European Library - Zaltbommel/Netherlands MCMLXXXVII

Acknowledgements: I am most grateful to those who have been kind enough to lend postcards and photographs for inclusion in this book, particularly fellow members of the Wealden Postcard Club. They are; Peter Allen, Lois and Gerald Huntley, Charles Kay, Jim Laker and Harry Veness. I am also most grateful to Ted Cook, Crawley Reference Library, and the late Pat Walls for allowing me to copy and reproduce material in their possession. Illustrations 25, 36 and 87 are reproduced by courtesy of Aerofilms Ltd, and 124 by courtesy of Pamlin Prints and Gatwick Airport Ltd. Approximately two thirds of the illustrations come from my own collection. John Goepel inspired me to action and those who kindly provided information and advice on the text included Mrs. Betty Allen, James Barrett, Richard Bucknall, Charles Harvey, Gerald Huntley, C.T. Johnson, Sir Norman and Lady Longley and Mrs. J.A. Shortall. My wife Patricia and son Charles have been most helpful in vetting my literary efforts, and I am especially grateful to Charles Kay of Crawley Reference Library for the interest, patience and care that he has taken in going over my text with a toothcomb – and sometimes guiding me gently back onto the rails! Quotations from 'The Brighton Road' by Charles G. Harper are reproduced by permission of the author's estate and Chatto & Windus: The Hogarth Press, and those from 'Highways and Byways in Sussex' by E.V. Lucas are reproduced by permission of Macmillans, London and Basingstoke. Other quotations are by kind permission of the Crawley Observer and Father Seamus Hester of the Friary, Crawley. Amongst over 100 sources I can only list those which I have turned to most frequently and these are: 'The Brighton Road' by Charles Harper (1892, 1906, 1922), 'The Crawley Doctors' by Dr. T.H. Martin (c1914), The Victoria County History of Sussex, vol. 7 (1940), 'Crawley As The Old Ones Knew It' by Mrs. H.C. Carman (1968), 'Down Memory Lane' by Jim Laker (1979), 'Crawley, Victorian New Town' by John Lowerson (1980), 'A Brief History of Three Bridges' by Jim Laker and Charles Kay (1983) – and many articles by the late W.J. Denman appearing in the Sussex and Surrey Courier and West Sussex County Times between 1929 and 1943. Above all I owe a debt of gratitude to the many Victorian, Edwardian and Georgian photographers and publishers of local views, especially those in the vicinity of Crawley, who included Lewis G. Ball, Mrs. Beard, Belchamber & Sons, W.T. Dean, Francis Frith & Co., Miss M. Phillips, Miss Newbery, J.W. Slator, P. Snelling and A.E. Willett. Their work is commemorated in these pages. *Postcard captions:* The original postcard captions have been retained wherever it has been sensible to do so. As there are many postcards bearing the caption 'Crawley High Street' or 'Three Bridges' etc., however, more explicit captions specifying buildings or location have been added where necessary, in the interests of clarity.

Michael Goldsmith, St. Margarets, October 1986

GB   ISBN 90 288 4525 9 / CIP

European Library in Zaltbommel/Netherlands publishes among other things the following series:

IN OLD PICTURE POSTCARDS *is a series of books which sets out to show what a particular place looked like and what life was like in Victorian and Edwardian times. A book about virtually every town in the United Kingdom is to be published in this series. By the end of this year about 300 different volumes will have appeared. 1,500 books have already been published devoted to the Netherlands with the title* **In oude ansichten.** *In Germany, Austria and Switzerland 650, 100 and 25 books have been published as* **In alten Ansichten;** *in France by the name* **En cartes postales anciennes** *and in Belgium as* **In oude prentkaarten** *and/or* **En cartes postales anciennes** *150 respectively 400 volumes have been published.*

For further particulars about published or forthcoming books, apply to your bookseller or direct to the publisher.

This edition has been printed and bound by Grafisch Bedrijf De Steigerpoort in Zaltbommel/Netherlands.

INTRODUCTION

Princess Elizabeth was 23 years old when she first visited the New Town of Crawley in Sussex and, on a bitterly cold day, opened the industrial estate, planted a maple tree on Crawley Green, inspected housing under construction and accepted a white toy dog for the young Prince Charles. The year was 1950, and I happen to remember the date – January 25th – because it was my 9th birthday. I was also aware that the village in which I had lived since birth was rapidly changing, and that no sooner had the words 'New Town' been broadcast on the radio than bulldozers moved in and the fields at the back of my home in Northgate were covered with bricks and mortar and windows – and childhood memories.

The New Town was one of eight built in a circle round London in the aftermath of the Second World War, and Crawley was chosen in preference to two other sleepy country villages in the vicinity, Holmwood near Dorking, and Crowhurst just north of Lingfield. It was a bold and imaginative piece of planning designed both to alleviate overcrowding in London – and, presumably, to make the Metropolis less of a concentrated target in any future bombing attack on England.

Ironically however, Crawley was not the totally new post-war creation that many subsequently seemed to think, but a village heading for its 800th anniversary and dating back to at least the days of 'bad King John'. Not only that but, by even greater irony, the future Queen was opening Crawley's second industrial area, the first having been developed – without any ceremony – over 2,000 years earlier, and lying buried under the neighbourhoods of Broadfields, Southgate and Bewbush. Excavations, which took place in 1972, revealed a series of over thirty furnaces designed to obtain iron ore from the local soil, and dating back to 190BC (the Late Iron Age), but subsequently taken over and expanded by the Romans in the 1st and 2nd centuries AD. Indeed by the time they vacated this primitive 'factory site' it extended for over 60 acres, and it is currently believed to be the largest of its kind yet discovered in Britain.

During the next 800 years the southern part of England was slowly settled by the invading tribes, and since the word Crawley has an ending of Old English or Saxon origin – the suffix *ley*, *leah*, *le* or *leigh* indicating a clearing in a wood or forest – it is not unreasonable to assume that a tiny colony – perhaps just a hut or two – was established here before the Normans came. Though Christianity arrived in Kent in 597AD it took another 400 years to penetrate the forests in this area however, and the first church to be established locally was at Worth in the early 11th century. It was followed by others at Slaugham (early 12th century) and Ifield (late 12th century) – and eventually by a chapel at Crawley, which was established as a 'chapel of ease' to the main church in Slaugham. Indeed, as late as 1536 it is referred to as 'Slaugham St. Mary cum Capella de Crawley' and the ecclesiastical ties were only completely severed in the 18th century!

In 1202-1203 Michael de Poynings was granted a licence to hold a weekly market at Crawley in return for paying King John 'a good Norway goshawk' – the first specific reference that we have to Crawley – though both Ifield and Worth gain mention as tiny communities in the Domesday Book (1086). The Poynings family managed to extend this permit in 1279 to include an Annual Fair as well – the Fair to be held on the eve and day of the Beheading of St. John The Baptist (28th August), and both markets and fairs would have been held on land surrounding the church, in accordance with the general custom. This practice was suddenly forbidden in 1285 however – during the reign of Edward I – and, deprived of their original site, the local events were forced out into what was to become the High Street. It is probably from this date therefore that the pattern of the village, as it remained down to 1947, was slowly established. (Markets and fairs often took the place of shops in those days of course, especially in smaller rural settlements.)

The period between 1250 and 1700 saw the spread of a number of large timber-framed dwellings and farmhouses northwards along the main street. These included the Ancient Priors and the Punch Bowl (names by which they are best known), the Tree – and Crawley's best known building, the George, the existence of the latter possibly resulting from the construction of a horse track between Reigate and Crawley c1450. Apart from the usual rural occupations there was a limited revival of iron working in Worth and Tilgate Forests from the 13th century onwards – and when the Wealden iron industry turned into a raging torrent in the 16th and 17th centuries, Crawley, stationed on the northern fringes of the forests, was inevitably involved. Indeed, until the industry faded away in the early 18th century, several ironmasters both lived and worked in the Crawley area, and names such as Leonard Gale and Roger Gratwick featured prominently in local history.

During the 18th century the Reigate to Crawley road was improved and turnpiked, and the discovery of Brighton by the Prince Regent in 1782 led to an eruption of traffic trundling from London to the coast and back. Situated 29 miles from the capital and 23 from Brighton, Crawley was the almost perfect 'half-way-house' on what could be a tiring coach journey – and posting houses such as the George, Rising Sun and White Hart did a roaring trade. (The George even acquired an annexe, in the middle of the street, to cope with the overflow!) The village also benefitted from two illegal activities which developed at around the same time – the Copthorne Smugglers Gang favouring both the Old White Hart (later Ancient Priors) and the Rising Sun as worthy headquarters – and thousands of well-heeled society followers descending on Crawley the night before a prizefight at nearby Crawley Down.

The arrival of the railway – at Three Bridges in 1841, and at Crawley seven years later – virtually killed the coaching trade, and at least one local inn, the Rising Sun, was forced to close. If life was quieter after the passing of the stagecoach though it certainly wasn't dull! Not only had the weekly markets been revived earlier in the century but the Crawley Fair had become a celebrated and spectacular twice yearly event, and the Old Crawley Sports Day provided the village with a famous annual horse race – attracting bookies and spectators from throughout the southeast. Easier and cheaper travel also brought a new breed of residents to the village too – commuters – and one of these was Mark Lemon, the first editor of Punch and a founder member of the local fire brigade. New houses sprang up to the west and south of the existing village and the High Street burst across the level crossing and spilled over into the Brighton Road – the 'Park Lane or Belgravia of Crawley' as Charles Harper put it in 1906.

By the time the First World War arrived Crawley had its own cinema and more than one garage, and there were almost 9,000 people living in the three communities of Worth, Crawley and Ifield. Heavy traffic to the south coast influenced the provision of a by-pass just before the Second World War, and a small aerodrome called Gatwick was established two miles north of Crawley in 1930. The latter was officially opened in 1936. Its elder companion, Gatwick Racecourse, closed just after the war however – having existed for over fifty years from its creation in the 1890's as a consequence of sporting hooliganism at Croydon. German bombs partly demolished Crawley's Baptist Chapel, an infant school and the new Post Office – but apart from that the village got off lightly – and acid bath murderer John George Haigh had a much more shocking impact on the community when he despatched his victims in West Green and was hanged for it at Lewes in August 1949. The creation of the New Town under a Parliamentary Act of 1946 had the most devastating effect of all though – and within ten years the shape of the village, which had taken centuries to evolve, was recast in an entirely new mould. Little did Princess Elizabeth appreciate the true significance of the occasion when she surveyed the broad and flag bedecked main street from a dais outside the George on a cold day in 1950!

I hope that you will enjoy this book for it is both a geographical and historical tour of the area, starting to the north with Crawley's Sun Inn, and stepping down 'the longest high street in the world' in the direction of The Half Moon at Hogs Hill. Pausing only for an Edwardian garden party we then survey Victorian developments in West Green, 'New Town' and East Park before heading in the direction of Three Bridges and Worth. Finally we circle back to take in the outlying districts of Tilgate, Ifield, Lowfield Heath and Gatwick. Many of the buildings and events described have passed into memory, but if you read the texts in order you will find a wealth of surprising detail about a little known corner of Sussex, and glimpse a past that deserves to be recaptured. I hope to expand on it in another book on 'The History of Crawley'.

1. *The George, Crawley.* Crawley's heyday, prior to becoming a New Town, was undoubtedly during the coaching era, from the 'discovery' of Brighthelmstone by the Prince of Wales (later George IV) in 1782, to the opening of the Brighton railway in 1841. Up to sixty stagecoaches a day rattled through the village in the great days of 'the Brighton Road'. Situated as it was though, almost half-way between London and Brighton, it was also a natural and most popular place to stop, both during the day and overnight. The existence of illegal prizefighting centres at Crawley Down and Copthorne, hamlets less than 5 miles away, proved an added attraction to most travellers. This view of the George Inn, Crawley's best known hostelry, was painted by the Victorian artist Alfred Robert Quinton (1853-1934) during the last quarter of the 19th century.

2. *The Sun Inn (1905).* From Victorian times the Sun Inn marked what was generally thought of as the northern boundary of the village. It was actually the second inn of this name, the original 'Rising Sun', which it succeeded, being situated some 250 yards further south opposite the Toll Gate. (See 4 and 5.) The building seen here was originally a private house, with the subsequent addition of a shop in the front garden, owned by Mr. Dean, 'Grocer & Dairyman'. The house was converted to an inn c1870. Woolborough Road, to the right of the picture, was formerly called Black Dog Lane and led to Black Dog Farm, of which only an outlying cottage survives, a pretty timber-framed and brick fronted house of the late 17th or early 18th century. The name Woolborough derived from members of the Wolbergh family, a William de Wolbergh being mentioned in 1296 and a Manor of Woolborough existing from 1488 to at least 1684.

3. *Albert Cottages (c1911)*. A pretty row of Victorian cottages demolished in 1983 to make way for a New Town office block. Constantly subject to flooding in the winter, the site was originally occupied by a cluster of huts known as 'The Magazine', reputedly dating back to the late 17th century. These were used for storage of powder and ammunition, both for the Army and the Preventitive Officers of H.M. Customs. The difficulty of travelling on country roads, especially in winter months in Sussex, made storage depots like this essential, and many more were to be found, dotted across the countryside. The location here was ironic, however, since the Customs' Men were collecting supplies only 100 yards away from the original 'Rising Sun Inn', one of Crawley's major smuggling centres! After their original use expired the Magazine huts were converted into cottages and, in turn, most of these were replaced by the 'Alberts' in the 1870's.

4. *The Rising Sun Inn (c1911)*. This was the view that greeted stagecoach passengers as they halted at Crawley's North Toll Gate on their way south to Brighton. The nearest building was the original 'Rising Sun Inn', one of three major coaching inns in the village. Together with the old White Hart (later the Ancient Priors) it was a haunt of the Copthorne Smugglers Gang, and in the late 18th and early 19th centuries illicit goods brought inland from Shoreham were hidden in a hollow hay rick next to the pond and Toll Cottage across the road. In 1833 the newly formed Crawley & Horsham Foxhounds stationed their kennels there, but with the arrival of the railway at Three Bridges in 1841 stagecoach trade collapsed and by 1846 the hostelry had closed its doors. The building then became a school called North House before being converted to a laundry c1928. It was demolished in 1980. Crawley doctor Timothy Martin occupied the far house until it became a café c1896. This was ultimately demolished in 1962.

5. *The North Gate Toll Cottage.* In 1696 an Act of Parliament was passed repairing the highway between Reigate and Crawley for the benefit of horsemen. In 1755 this road was widened and surfaced to take coach traffic, and the road through Crawley itself was turnpiked in 1770. The North Toll Gate & Cottage probably dated from this time therefore, the latter standing on 'common land' with a large pond next to it used for watering the horses. Following the introduction of faster stagecoaches in 1823 up to sixty coaches a day passed through the Toll Gate in the summer months. When the railway arrived in 1841 however, the number was immediately reduced to four in each direction and, as in many other areas of Sussex, the local Turnpike Trust was gradually forced to concede defeat. The North Crawley Toll Gate was finally removed c1870, the last attendant being Mrs. Agate, a sister of Sarah Robinson, founder of two major schools in the village.

The Old Tree, Crawley.

6. *The Old Tree, Crawley (c1916).* The ancient elm on the left was Crawley's most celebrated landmark. Not only was it at least 300 years old when this photo was taken but in its prime was estimated to have been twice the height of Crawley's Church tower and some 12 feet in diameter. Early in the 19th century a brick floored room was created in the base and soldiers were sometimes billeted there en route to the garrison in Brighton. A poor woman was also reported to have given birth there in 1823. The house facing it was appropriately called 'The Tree' and was a timber-framed building of the late 14th century, though embedded and faced in brick by subsequent owners. In 1798 it became home and surgery to Doctor Robert Smith, a young man of 24 and the only doctor for miles around. On his death in 1828 he was succeeded by his son Tom, who carried on the practice for the next 34 years and was remembered as '*the* most respected man in the village'.

7. *Old Tree & Rectory Lodge (c1907).* Thomas Smith's spell as local doctor was notable for the year 1833 when he was joined for a time by 17 year old medical student, John Leech, soon to become a celebrated artist. After Smith's death in 1862 his five daughters continued to live at the house and, when the last one passed away in 1935 'The Tree' was 'restored' and today serves as offices for local voluntary services. The barn which stood behind the house was probably of 15th century origin, and recent study has suggested that this building, which was jettied, might have been a medieval meeting place, with shops below and the main chamber above. It was removed during construction of the New Town and is now on display at the Weald and Downland Museum near Chichester. The famous elm was not so lucky though since it was badly damaged in storms of 1883 and 1935 and gradually rotted away. The Victorian Rectory standing at the top of the drive was demolished in the 1950's.

Albany Temperance Hotel.
London Road.

8. *Albany Temperance Hotel – London Road (1907).* Just across the way from Crawley's celebrated elm lay the Albany Temperance Hotel. 'Temperance' has a rather quaint ring to it nowadays, but in Victorian and Edwardian times there was a strong reaction to the widespread drunkenness of the 18th and early 19th centuries, and many 'Temperance' movements were established. Crawley residents evidently had vigorous views on 'the demon drink' and Crawley Temperance marches and banners are continually to be found in turn of the century photographs (cf photo 59). Tom Terry, who ran the Albany Hotel at this date, was clearly a pillar of Edwardian respectability, and his round form and white straw hat were most likely to be found in the sedate tea gardens, with their colourful umbrellas, which lay behind the hedge on the left. In due course the hotel was demolished and, in 1938, the Embassy Cinema was opened on the site. (Now converted into three Canon cinemas.)

LONDON ROAD — CRAWLEY

9. *London Road, Crawley (c1904)*. Of all the pictures in this book I think that this is my favourite! With the Temperance Hotel on the left, the 'elm' in the background, and Crawley Green on the right we are, as one writer put it 'twenty-nine miles only from London, and yet soothed with peaceful rurality' (Charles Harper, The Brighton Road, 1892). The writer of the postcard obviously shared a similar feeling too, informing a friend in Walthamstow: 'Such a lovely day, we are enjoying it immensely. 1.30, just had our dinner.' Who would believe that there are now traffic lights in front of the Albany Tea Gardens, that the tree on the left has been replaced by the Bingo Club & Bowling Alley, and that the trackway on the right is now 'The Boulevard' and leads to a gigantic modern shopping centre?

10. *Old house, Crawley (c1906).* How many New Town residents know that Crawley used to have a farm in its main street I wonder? The building on the right, which lay 50 yards south of 'The Tree', is familiar to present day inhabitants of the town as The National Westminster Bank. At one time, however, it used to be a farmhouse, 'Michells', and up to the 1890's had a range of farm buildings including granary, stables, barn etc. in full use on its northern and eastern sides. It was the biggest retail dairy farm in the vicinity and its herd of cows were a regular sight in the High Street as they crossed 'to pastures new'. The farmhouse was built in the early 15th century and, in its prime, was a classic 'Wealden hall-house', with timber framing, wattle and daub infilling and jettied overhangs. Such houses were too good for ordinary villagers it should be said, even in medieval times, and this one was probably specially constructed for the original farmer, or perhaps even an 'up and coming' local trader.

11. *Old house, Crawley (c1905).* The first 'known' owner of the building was Robert Hall of Ifield, who held it in 1789. His son Richard inherited it in 1792, and as he and his wife Sarah were childless, it passed to two nominated 'co-heirs' on his death in 1825. When it ceased to be a farmhouse later in the 19th century it was divided into two cottages known as 'The Old House' and 'Tyler's Cottage' and it is in this state that it can be seen in the photo above. (Stephen Tyler was a small scale dairyman and haulage contractor – having three cows and one horse!) Originally the house consisted of an enormous hall, with two-storey service wings at either end, but the whole house was converted into two floors in the 16th century, an extra wing being added at the northern end. The building is also partly jettied (ie the upper floor is wider than and projects out over the lower floor), and the northern jetty is clearly visible in this picture.

12. *Ye Olde Punch Bowle (c1935).* In 1928 one half of the property was sold to Mr. and Mrs. Charles Merser, and having acquired the other half soon after, Mr. Merser organised the 'restoration' of the entire building in 1929. Much of the earlier lath and plaster was stripped away, many of the original beams were re-exposed, greatly needed repairs were carried out – and in no time at all the reunified house was on the market again, this time emerging as 'Ye Olde Punch Bowle', a pleasant roadside café. In this guise it performed yeoman service for nearly twenty years, numbering amongst its unsuspecting customers the figure of John George Haigh, the Crawley acid-bath murderer, tried and hanged for his crimes in 1949. Eventually, with the coming of the New Town, the sedate old building was acquired for use by the National Provincial Bank – in 1952 – and is now a secure home for the re-named National Westminster Bank.

13. *Old houses (c1911).* Next door to the future 'Punch Bowle' (seen on the left) was another old house, probably of 17th century origin and also timber-framed, though faced with brick in late Victorian times. At the time of this photo, in 1911, it had been divided into three cottages – but has long since been demolished. Beyond was an 18th century house and beyond that 'The Brewery' (later Brewery Shades), yet another 15th century timber-framed 'hall house', though almost totally disguised behind a 19th century frontage. Stretching in front of all these houses is Crawley Green, a 150 yard strip of grassland accompanying the road all the way from 'The Tree' to the widening of the road just before the White Hart. There were two occasions when the 'Green' was submerged with unaccustomed activity. The first was on 'The Old Crawley Sports Day'. (See 42 text.) The second was on the occasion of Crawley Fair.

14. *Crawley Fair (May 1905)*. The Fair took place in May and September each year, and this end of the main street was divided between animals and entertainment. The traditional 'horse fair' took place between the George Hotel and Rose Cottages, and the animals seen here were waiting to be raced up and down the road for the benefit of prospective buyers. At the May Fair too, the Green was where pigs, sheep and poultry were penned for display. Above all though, it was the place for pleasure! The swing boats outside Tompsett's were accompanied by stalls selling brandy snaps and humbugs, by cocoanut shies, fortune tellers, gambling booths, 'Fat Ladies', dwarves, 'Living Skeletons', 'The Wild Man of Borneo', the 'Battle of Waterloo' – and many others. Across the road there was a pleasure fair in the Town Meadow, with a steam organ, a roundabout wound by hand, and naptha flares for lighting over the stalls. 'Fair Day' was sheer magic! (See 44-47 also.)

15. *Crawley, looking south (c1905).* Charles Harper, whose 'Brighton Road' was first published in 1892, wrote of Crawley: *The extreme length of its long street, together with the quaint cottages and their homely front gardens, give the place so pleasing an air of rusticity, that, inconstant traveller! you vote it the compeer of Merstham in its old world charm. The large and long patches of grass that take up so considerable a selvedge of Crawley Street seem to speak with eloquence of those dead days of coaching necessity, when even this generous width of roadway cannot have been an inch too wide for the traffic that crowded the village when Crawley was a stage at which every coach stopped… Down the street the air was full of the scent of those old fashioned flowers that gladden the heart by their artless beauty…* Tempis fugit! The last of the houses on the right, including the aptly named 'Rose Cottages', were demolished in the early days of the New Town.

16. *The First Stock Exchange Walk (1903)*. Seven years after Crawley residents witnessed the passage of the first motor cars on their way to Brighton ('Motor Car Day' 14th November 1896 – the day the car was legalised in this country), the first of the celebrated 'Stock Exchange Walks' also passed through the village. E.V. Lucas, writing in 1904 commented: *One would be hard put to think of a less desirable existence than that of dwelling on a dusty road and continually seeing people hurrying either from Brighton to London or from London to Brighton… And not only travellers on wheels; for since the fashion for walking came in, Crawley has had new excitements, or monotones, in the shape of walking stockbrokers, walking butchers, walking auctioneers' clerks, walking Austrians pushing their families in wheelbarrows, walking bricklayers carrying hods of bricks, walking acrobats on stilts, – all striving to get to Brighton within a certain time.*

E.F. BROAD Winner of the First Prize
Accompanied by JENNY WALTERS, 24 hours Bicycle Champion of the World

17. *The Great Stock Exchange Walk (1903)*. The inaugural Stock Exchange Walk was held on 1st May 1903. It was won by E.F. Broad, seen here passing Crawley's 18th century 'Rose Cottages' and the Regency bow fronted elegance of Camfields the Tailors. Broad reached Brighton in 9 hours and 30 minutes and conditions were so atrocious that he arrived at Brighton Aquarium 'with his legs plastered in solid mud up to the knees'. Clearly such treks could be arduous and the following year Lucas waspishly noted that 'At Handcross, lower on the road, the numbers diminish, but every competitor seems to be able to reach Crawley, perhaps because the railway station adjoins the high road'! Perhaps it was no coincidence that Norman Wisdom, the comedian, was seen participating in the Stock Exchange Walk close to Crawley station in the film 'One Good Turn' (1954)!

High Street, Crawley (Looking South)

18. *High Street, looking south (c1903).* This is the view that greeted the newly arrived traveller from London. *Its most striking peculiarity is the extraordinary width of the road; and the next most remarkable thing is the bygone impudence of some forgotten land-snatchers who seized plots in midst of this street, broad enough for a market place, and built houses on them. By what slow, insensible degrees these sites, doubtless originally those of market-stalls, were stolen, records do not tell us; but we may imagine the movable stalls replaced by fixed wooden ones, and those in course of time giving place to more substantial structures… until the present houses… sealed and sanctified the long-drawn tale of grab.* (Charles Harper, 'The Brighton Road', 1906.) The most peculiar fact of all though, which Harper didn't know, was that the George Hotel, on the right, was in the parish of Ifield, and its 'Annexe', in the centre, was in the parish of Crawley!

19. *Guy Fawkes Bonfire, Crawley High Street (1910)*. Lower Square, encompassed by the George Inn, the George Annexe and the White Hart, was the site of the 'Guy Fawkes night' bonfire, held on 5th November each year. Elaborate preparations were made in Victorian and Edwardian times and a 'Bonfire Society' met regularly at the White Hart from September onwards. The members, or 'Bonfire Boys' as they were called, worked hard to create large balls of tow, which were then immersed in paraffin for several weeks before being wired into triangular iron frames. Placed on the ends of long poles these were then ignited, with spectacular effect, in 'torchlight processions' on the way to the bonfire. This picture, taken in 1910, marked the end of an era though, for with the introduction of tarmacadam road surfaces there was a real danger of setting the street alight and, in 1911, the celebrations were transferred to a field behind the White Hart.

Ye Olde George, Crawley. 1764.

20. *Ye Olde George, Crawley (1789!)* Crawley's most celebrated building, the George Inn, traditionally dates from 1615, the year carved on a fireplace near the entrance. It is mentioned in the will of Richard Covert, who died in 1579 though ('The George worth 40s, held of John Shirley'), and most experts agree that it probably originated in the 15th century. Indeed its existence may well have resulted from the construction of a horse track from Reigate to Crawley c1450. This aquatint, by Thomas Rowlandson, is the oldest picture of Crawley we possess, and first appeared in a journal titled 'An Excursion to Brighthelmstone in 1789'. Historically the scene is interesting since, although the George itself is now much altered, one of the houses in the middle of the upper street is already in existence, the famous gallows straddling the road is still to be seen, and the sale of horses outside the Inn remained a traditional part of Crawley Fairs right down to the present century.

21. *George Hotel, Crawley (Victorian photo).* Up to 1755 only horsemen could use the narrow causeway between Reigate and Crawley, but the fortunes of the George were boosted in that year when the route was widened, turnpiked, and wheeled traffic finally permitted. When the Prince Regent (later George IVth) 'discovered' Brighthelmstone in 1782, turning it into a fashionable resort, the road through Crawley soared in popularity, and being 29 miles from Big Ben, and 'half-way house' on what was initially an eight hour journey, the George began to do a roaring trade. Before long up to sixty coaches a day passed through the village and 'The George Inn' became a familiar place at which to dine, change horses, or stay overnight. Famous visitors included Lord Nelson (whose sister lived at Handcross) and Queen Victoria, and one elderly resident testified that she had seen no less than three reigning sovereigns enter the hostelry.

The George Hotel, Crawley.

22. *The George Hotel, looking north (c1916).* The presence of illegal prizefighting 'mills' at both Crawley Down and Copthorne, during the late 18th and first half of the 19th centuries, provided another reason for visiting Crawley, and the George was inundated with visitors on the eve of every fight. Conan Doyle immortalised the scene in his novel 'Rodney Stone'. *And then, at last, we saw the formless mass of the huge Crawley elm looming before us in the gloom, and there was the broad village street with the glimmer of the cottage windows, and the high front of the Old George Inn, glowing from every door and pane and crevice, in honour of the noble company who were to sleep within that night.* World heavyweight champion John L. Sullivan was one real life visitor, world bantamweight champion 'Pedlar Palmer' trained here, and Tom Cribb liked Crawley so much that he lived here!

23. *The George Annexe, looking north (c1923).* The arrival of the railway at Three Bridges in 1841 caused a rapid decline in Crawley's stagecoach trade, and when the last of the George's 'postboys' departed in 1887, an era finally came to a close. In its heyday, however, the George was so busy that it took over extra premises, uniquely situated, right in the middle of the High Street! The 'Annexe', as it was called, was probably built in the late 18th or early 19th century, and was reputed to have been erected by a member of the Snelling family as a candle factory! Its most famous occupant was Queen Victoria, who stayed there when her carriage broke down. In later years, however, the ground floor was occupied by Mrs. Elms, a lady dentist and owner of two enormous bloodhounds, much in demand by the local police who possessed no such animals of their own! The George Annexe was eventually demolished in 1933 and replaced by a car park.

24. *The Old Saddler's Shop (Victorian photo)*. This venerable business numbered King George IV, King William IV and Queen Victoria amongst its clients and had been in existence since at least 1721. It was sited two doors south of the George, on the corner of Ifield Road, and, as you might expect of a coaching village, specialised in everything connected with horses. (You can see some of the wares in this lovely picture.) It also offered sporting goods, and an early owner, Nathaniel Miller, had a bit of a reputation as a local vet. His son, Milton, was also keen on animals and was particularly fond of dog fighting, a sport that was both fashionable and popular in Victorian times. On one celebrated occasion Milton matched his dog 'Rattler' against a tiger in Crabbet Park and won, though the dog subsequently died and was buried in a special dogs' cemetery on the estate. Miller's was eventually demolished early in 1939.

CRAWLEY. FROM THE AIR

25. *Crawley from the air (1929)*. A classical view of Crawley High Street, looking north, with its two sets of buildings marooned in the centre of the road, like ships at anchor! Arriving from London your vehicle would enter Lower Square (top of picture) and, after passing the George Annexe and the central or Market Square, would then come to a second group of buildings known just as 'The Square'. The aerial view shows clearly that the latter was an amalgamation of past generations of houses – and may even have included a farmhouse. (See 35.) For many years the western side of the street, including the George Hotel (top left), lay in Ifield parish, whilst the eastern side and buildings in the middle of the road formed part of the parish of Crawley. It was only in 1928 in fact, just before this plane flew over the village, that the two parishes at last merged in local government.

26. *Lower Square (1905).* Descending from the 'bird's eye view' in the previous picture to the eastern side of the High Street (and still looking in the same direction) we find a row of homely two storey buildings at the northern end, opposite Lower Square. Herrett's, on the right, was a small scale dairy run by Miss Herrett and her father, and the good lady had the reputation of being a bit of a tartar, putting the fear of God into more than one young schoolboy in her day! The premises later became a restaurant and cake shop. Johnson's next door, boasted of tea gardens coupled with cycle repairs, a very astute combination of activities in my opinion since the need for emergency attention to one's bike invariably produced a handy excuse for a spot of rest and refreshment! In front of both businesses ran the hitching rails for the White Hart, the next building along and, in its heyday, one of Crawley's three major coaching inns.

27. *The White Hart (c1903).* This is an 18th century inn, built of brick and possessing a tiled roof. Though of later construction than the George and Rising Sun it was erected in time for the grand days of coaching in the late 18th and first half of the 19th centuries, and was a major staging post with stables for 180 horses and a very useful pond! The White Hart was also headquarters for a fortnightly corn market, which was a going concern from around 1800 until it petered out in 1883. Crawley's first post office was founded there in 1802, and its Benefit Society, started in 1827, was the oldest of all 'friendly societies' in the district. (Clubs formed to encourage thrift and mutual assistance.) Crawley Feast or 'Club' Day was held there once a year too, a mammoth affair starting at 10am with a parade to church, a business meeting, a 3 hour lunch in a marquee on the White Hart Field, athletic contests in the afternoon and a concluding toast at 9.00pm.

28. *High Street, Crawley (c1910).* The old house to the right of the stagecoach in the previous picture had been demolished by the time this photo was taken, and a modern building with dormer windows erected in its place. Beyond, you can glimpse the timber-framing of the former 'Old White Hart', later known as 'The Ancient Priors'. Quite how the village came to have two inns called the White Hart, within 70 yards of each other, no one knows, but the one at the far end was certainly the older of the two. This view reminds me of Conan Doyle's book 'Rodney Stone' incidentally, where Crawley High Street is described on the morning of a big fight at Crawley Down. *The night before* (the vehicles) *had lain with their wheels interlocking and their shafts under each other's bodies… from the old church to the Crawley Elm, spanning the road five deep for a good half-mile in length. Now the grey village street lay before us almost deserted save by a few women and children. Men, horses, carriages – all were gone.*

29. *The Ancient Prior's House (c1925).* Until it lost its licence as a beerhouse in 1881 this magnificent timber-framed building was known as 'The Old White Hart', and was the original inn of that name. Though experts agree that the present house dates from about 1450, it is likely that it replaced an earlier construction, since a dwelling is mentioned here as far back as 1250, in the reign of Henry III. This would have been around the time St. John's Church was built and, from its proximity to the latter, it is quite possible that the two were associated. Indeed it may well have been the Chantry House for Nicholas Wordsworth, 'Chantry Priest' of Crawley, who directed in his will of 1532 that 'my house shall be sold, which I did buy of Mr. Thomas Mychele'. In the early 1700's it was also in the ownership of Leonard Gale, the ironmaster, who may have lived here for a time, and through whom it passed to the Blunt family.

30. *High Street, Crawley (c1906).* During the late 18th and early 19th centuries 'The Old White Hart', like the 'Rising Sun' nearby, became a celebrated haunt for the Copthorne Smugglers Gang, who brought illicit goods inland from Shoreham. Though talk of subterranean passages and hidey holes has always been greatly exaggerated, three have been authenticated; a secret bedchamber over the dairy reached by pushing one of several innocuous hooks in the passage from the kitchen; a hiding place for two men at the rear of the giant kitchen fireplace; and a secret room 6 ft by 4ft in size, with the remains of a staircase. (Uncovered during renovations in the autumn of 1984.) Later in the 19th century it was not only an inn but also housed a shop next to the front entrance, accommodated the local barber Fred Russell in an upstairs room, and was associated with Crosskeys Farm which lay at its back door. The farm ceased to function as such around 1875.

31. *The Ancient Prior's Café (c1935)*. After it lost its drinks licence in 1881 the inn became a Temperance Hotel for a while (to which Lord Kitchener was a visitor), and then the property of Samuel Collier Burgess, grocer and house furnisher. Just before the First World War it was acquired by Mr. G.A. Parkhurst, an enterprising antiques dealer, and he it was who had the brainwave of renaming it 'The Ancient Priest's House', subtly upgraded to 'The Ancient Prior's House' during the war, a name by which it is now universally known (see 29). The lovely medieval hall-house, with its elegant double gables, was restored by Mr. Parkhurst in 1927 and many of the original beams were once again revealed, though the superb roof of Horsham stone slabs was, quite correctly, left untouched. (See above.) Soon afterwards it became a café and restaurant, and has remained such down to the present day – a recent owner being Crawley man Alan Minter, the world middleweight boxing champion.

32. *Junction of High Street and Ifield Road (1905).* Opposite the Ancient Prior's lies the entrance to Ifield Road, guarded down to 1939 by the Old Saddler's Shop (see 24). The nearest corner has an interesting history since at one time it is believed that an oak tree grew on the spot, which the Lord of the Manor of Ifield rented out as a hitching post on Fair Days. When the Ifield Road was created, apparently in the 18th century, the remains of the tree were thought to have been incorporated in the wall, and a large ring inserted, into which the Lord of the Manor, or his nominee, placed an oak bough on Fair Days, thereby entitling him to sell beer to an appreciative public! Up to the 18th century the principal road leading west was Small's Lane incidentally, a track which left the High Street just north of the present Bowling Alley and proceeded via Goffs Hill, Bewbush and Colgate to Horsham. By 1795, however, the main entrance to the 'Horsham Road' was the one pictured here and Small's Lane itself fell into disuse.

33. *High Street, looking south (c1903).* Standing at the entrance to Ifield Road, but this time looking south, the building reputed to contain the oak tree is the one on the right. At the turn of the century it was occupied by Smith and Sons, 'grocers, drapers, house furnishers and butchers', and is a much older building than it appears, being a 16th century timber-framed house which originally had a jettied overhang. It was revamped in the 18th century and the shops were inserted in early Victorian times. 'Spenny' Spencer Smith had a farm and slaughterhouse a little to the west and Spenser's Road, Crawley, is named after him. His second wife was also memorable as she possessed two thumbs on each hand! Up to the end of the First World War the room over the butcher's shop on the left was used by the YMCA for its Sunday religious meetings. Latterly however, in the 1940's and 1950's, it only echoed to the hum of a local dentist's drill.

34. *Crawley & Ifield Co-operative Society (c1907).* 'Co-operators' were workers who banded together to form local societies selling bread, groceries, dairy produce, linen etc., to members through their own shops, profits being divided in the form of annual dividends. Not surprisingly they were regarded with horror and distrust by the establishment. The Crawley and Ifield Co-operative Society was created in 1888 and its initial membership of 103 was drawn mainly from the ranks of local building and railway workers. (Curiously although a cart is listed in the assets after twelve months – a horse does not appear for another nine years!). Early attempts to establish a bakery in Crawley and a branch in Three Bridges both resulted in failure and the first manager resigned in 1892, after a heated scene at the quarterly meeting. The Society ultimately prospered though and new branches were eventually opened, in Horley in 1926, and in Three Bridges in 1928.

35. *The Square, Crawley, looking north (c1922).* The history of the southernmost block of buildings occupying the middle of Crawley's High Street is only sketchily recorded. Rowlandson's engraving (see 20) published in 1789, shows one house already 'in situ' on the northern side, and the same house, devoid of shops, is still clearly visible in photos taken over seventy years later. With the surge in building that followed the arrival of the railway other houses were added in the second half of the 19th century, and by the 1860's Fred Russell, barber and local historian, was running a general 'emporium' at this end of the block – which came to be known as 'The Square'. Henty's, one of the earliest local banks, also had a branch here. The houses and shops on the right of the Square had their backyards inside it by the way, and at one time there were broad wooden steps on the left, leading to workshops. The Square was demolished in 1958.

36. *Central Crawley and St. John's Church (1929)*. Medieval road conditions were probably responsible both for the width of Crawley's High Street and for the two blocks of houses which were sited in the middle of it! In olden times Sussex roads were notorious for becoming waterlogged and impassable in winter months, and the track through Crawley was unlikely to have been an exception. In consequence traffic might well have skirted round the edges and, in doing so, the road gradually became broader. The vacant central area would then have been taken over by market stallholders during the drier months and, in the course of time, temporary seasonal holdings were replaced by more permanent ones. St. John's Church, on the right, was undeniably the hub of the earliest village though, and the original weekly markets would have been held on land surrounding it. With the banning of fairs from churchyards in 1285 however, the tiny hamlet probably had just the impetus it needed to expand.

37. *Crawley Parish Church (c1907).* St. John's Church is the earliest building known to exist in Crawley and when first established in the mid-13th century was a 'chapel of ease' to the main church at Slaugham. By the end of Henry VIII's reign, 300 years later, it was referred to as 'The ould chappell of Crawley with above one hundred houselyng people', and was clearly the centre of a parish in its own right. The tower which dominates it was added in the middle of the 15th century, but the history of three curious figures carved on it (one of which is John the Baptist) appears to have been lost. So too does the origin of the inscription on a beam inside: 'Man yn wele be war (in good fortune beware), for wardly good maketh man blynde, Be war be for whate comyth be hynde.' The church was much restored in 1845 and 1880, and a clock, costing £250 and funded by public subscription, was added in 1901, as a monument to the reign of Queen Victoria.

High Street, Crawley.

38. *High Street, Crawley looking north (c1909).* The demolition of three cottages in front of the church enabled the creation of a new gateway from church to High Street, first opened in 1898 and just visible on the right. Previous access had been solely by way of Church Path, a small alleyway running between the two gabled buildings in the foreground. The nearest of these two buildings was, for many years, known as the Albany Coffee and Dining Rooms, a celebrated cyclist's stop on the Brighton Road, and still in use as such in 1893. (It may even have been a halting place for J.H. Herbert when he cycled backwards to Brighton in 1895 in the unenviable time of 7 hours 45 minutes!) The second gabled edifice was opened as a draper's shop by John Cheal in 1800, and his son, who attended a Quaker school in Yorkshire, recorded completing his education at 15, just in time to hear the bells of Crawley Church ring out in celebration of Napoleon's defeat at Waterloo.

39. *Band Competition, Crawley (1907).* Victorian and Edwardian Crawley had an exceptionally strong musical tradition, and when it was the turn for our village to play host in area competitions absolutely everyone turned out! The Annual Southern Counties Amateur Band Association Contest was held in Crawley in 1907, 1913, 1922 and 1935 and here we see the Redhill Town Band passing between The Square and the new church entrance in 1907. Look at the people crowded in the windows, squatting on the rooftops and standing on the balconies! Back in the 1870's the local Fire Brigade Band ruled the roost, but before long it was joined by the West Crawley Silver Band, the Town Band, Military Band and Temperance Band – and of course the Salvation Army, whose services took place every Sunday night near the signal box! The Hazeldene Orchestra met at Moses Nightingale's house in the Brighton Road and there was even an operatic society, a harmonic society and a minstrel group!

40. *Crawley Band, 12th June 1905.* Of all the local bands, premier position was unquestionably occupied by the Town Band, a brass and reed ensemble which rehearsed twice a week and performed in the High Street on Saterday nights – to the delight, or consternation, of one and all! It was under the patronage of the Nix family from Tilgate, and its efforts were duly rewarded when it carried off the Southern Counties' Championship in 1913. No mean achievement for a small village, and the 36 members of the band and their conductor H.G. Melville had every reason to be proud! Crawley Silver Prize Band also won the Southern Counties' Championship in their section in 1925.

41. *Band Competition, Crawley, 20th May 1907.* The total population for Crawley, Ifield and Worth in the 1901 census was 8,121, but I think a good proportion of them are in the High Street on this occasion, don't you? The building with the double gables in the centre was called Vine Cottage and Crawley's most celebrated resident, Mark Lemon, first editor of Punch, lived there from 1857 until his death in 1870. It is often said that Lemon was frequently visited by his friend Charles Dickens whilst in Crawley, but this is sheer nonsense since the two men fell out very badly indeed just after Lemon moved here, and were not even on speaking terms for the next nine years! John Tenniel, the original illustrator of 'Alice in Wonderland', *was* a close friend though and Lemon's 8 year old daughter Kate served as the model for the famous drawings of the heroine. Lemon's most lasting contribution to Crawley life was the founding of a local Fire Brigade – an organisation which inevitably formed its own band!

42. *Crawley Band Sports – The Baby Show!* Did you know that Crawley used to be the centre for a major horse racing event; that bookies and pickpockets used to come down from London in droves; that there used to be a cycling race from Crawley Station to Lowfield Heath and back, with throngs of spectators lining the route; that men came from all over the south of England to compete in the athletic events, with valuable monetary prizes? No? Well, it's true, and all these things took place just once a year, on 'Old Crawley Sports Day', a mammoth event held throughout Victorian times, until it finally died the death in 1893. (The Band Sports cameoed here were but an Edwardian echo of a famous event!) The main horse race on this great day was the Crawley Cup, run over 1½ miles for a prize of £12 12s (1885), the racecourse being just south of Tushmore Lane. The athletic events took place on meadows to the east of the old tollgate, and Crawley Green was covered with booths, marquees and sideshows for the day!

43. *Smith's Stores (c1929).* Look at the dolls and teddy bear knocking back 'Shredded Wheat' in the right hand corner. You don't find 'promotions' like this any more do you? This shop was on the western side of the High Street, on the northern corner of Post Office Road and, in the earliest part of the century, used to belong to Ockenden, the tailor (see plate 41 taken in 1907). (The Ockenden family also ran the brewery just round the corner.) Just before the war it was taken over by Mrs. Bertha Smith, who ran the butcher's shop next door and also a draper's in Post Office Road, and the conversion of the traditional village tailor's shop into a general stores somehow seemed symptomatic of a changing era. Even though the window display may seem old-fashioned by today's standards for instance it is so 'modern' that it would have been unthinkable in Victorian times!

44. *Crawley Fair (1905)*. The highlight of village life in Victorian and Edwardian Crawley was the 'Fair', held in May and September of every year. On 'Fair Day' (when it was always reputed to rain), the place was awash with farmers and gypsies, tinkers and showmen, all competing for the undivided attentions of the spellbound rural community. As a rule it was 'business in the morning, pleasure after lunch' and commercial transactions were dominated by the cattle market in the Upper Square (seen here) and the horse fair by the George Hotel. Smaller livestock were herded in pens on Crawley Green. The Middle and Lower Squares were occupied by machinery, roundabouts, shooting galleries and boxing booths, whilst outside the White Hart rows of small stallholders eagerly sold ornaments, sweets, toys and fried fish. From Lower Square northwards, entertainments of all kinds gladdened the eye, including swingboats on the green and a pleasure fair in the meadow opposite.

45. *Crawley Fair (1905).* The history of the 'Fair' and market dated back to the 13th century. In 1202-1203 Michael de Poynings was granted a licence to hold a weekly market at Crawley in return for paying King John 'a good Norway goshawk'. Then, in 1279, Luke de Poynings (probably a grandson or great grandson of the original applicant) succeeded in amplifying the permit and was officially given leave to hold an annual Fair as well as the Friday market – the Fair to be held on the eve and day of the Beheading of St. John The Baptist (28th August). Both the Fair and market would have been held on land surrounding the local church in their earliest years (less than 100 yards from this scene), and the choice of date was almost certainly a matter of finding a day appropriate to the name of the church – St. John's. In 1285, however, it became an offence to hold fairs in churchyards, and it is probably from this date that the embryo village of Crawley began to expand.

46. *Crawley Fair (1905)*. All medieval fairs and markets were under the control of the lord of the manor, whose steward presided over a 'Pie Powder Court', a temporary local court empowered to resolve disputes and punish anyone breaking the rules. (Pie Powder being a corruption of the French, 'pieds poudreux' or the 'dusty footed'.) This court would have met in the 'Tolbooth' or 'tolsey', an early administrative office. In 1545 the manor of Crawley, and therefore the rights to the Fair and markets, passed from the Poynings family to the Shurleys, and both rights are documented as belonging to the Shurley family in 1579. It is likely that the market lapsed during the next two centuries, however, since only the Fair is listed in 'Owen's New Book of Fairs', published in 1792. By 1832 though James Pigot was noting that 'the market, which is very small, is held on Thursday', and the Reverend T. W. Horsfield writing in 1835 recorded that fairs were held 'for horned cattle' on 8th May and 29th September.

47. *Crawley Fair (1905)*. A minor change occurred in the 1860's when the date for the September Fair was brought forward to the 9th. 1896 marked a turning point though, for in that year the newly formed parish councils of Ifield and Crawley set up a joint body to control the Fairs, an essential step as the High Street lay in both parishes. Standard charges were then introduced, alongside a regulation preventing carts or shows entering the village before 6 pm on the eve of a Fair. In Edwardian times the arrival of the motor car began to clash with the increased frequency of the cattle market and an auction was introduced in a field behind the George to alleviate the problem. Ultimately though trouble with gipsies forced a showdown and the Fairs were abolished from the streets in September 1923. By 1938 only the May Fair was still in existence, in a much impoverished form off the High Street, and with the coming of the Second World War, disappeared altogether.

Crawley. High Street.

48. *Upper Square (1903).* This was the scene when the bands had departed, the drovers had herded cattle to new homes, the farm labourers had found new masters – and the Edwardian village returned to its slumbers. The message on the back of this postcard says it all: 'Miss Studd and I had tea here, at Gravely's, on the right of the photo.' (The building mid-right with single gable.) Gravely's was actually a baker's, with a tea shop at the front and the bakehouse at the back, and the business was one of the oldest in Crawley, having been established in 1780. Harry Gravely, who owned the business at the time (and who always wore a traditional baker's hat and apron) was succeeded by his son-in-law J.A. Hill in 1913. 'Handy' Court, the local signwriter, occupied the 16th century premises two doors to the left of Gravely's by the way, and if he were alive today I'm sure he'd like to know that his great grandson is married to Margaret Smith, the former Wimbledon Tennis Champion.

49. *Junction of High Street and Three Bridges Road (1920's).* Standing in an almost identical position to that occupied by Francis Frith's photographer in plate 48, but this time facing south, the cars on the right are heading towards Crawley's ill-famed level crossing. The horse and cart on the other hand are parked on the corner of the road leading east to Three Bridges. Originally called Worth Lane this then became Three Bridges Road and is now known as Haslett Avenue, after Dame Caroline Haslett, a native of Worth and the first woman to receive training as an electrical engineer. Except for Penfold's all the shops at this junction were demolished in the late 1950's, and the site is now disfigured by a concrete traffic island, of which, aesthetically at least, the local authorities should be rather ashamed!

50. *Junction of High Street and Three Bridges Road, detail (1920's).* I couldn't resist including this enlargement from the previous picture since the clothes, the hats (worn in bright sunshine), the style of the shop fronts, and even the horse waiting calmly outside the corn merchant's, capture an era in English history that has passed by forever.

51. *John Penfold & Sons (c1895).* This picture dates from late Victorian times and shows the shop belonging to John Penfold and Sons, 'Corn and Coal Merchants, Garden and Agricultural Seedsmen'. It was originally thought that this was a 17th century house but during extensive conversions in 1983 it was revealed as a timber-framed structure with wattle and daub infilling, and clearly of earlier date. It was also seen to possess a beautiful staircase dating from 1635. Penfold's were in business by 1878 and the stables needed for the delivery horses lay to the rear of the house, and were reached from Three Bridges Road (or Worth Lane as it was first known). John Penfold was a Parish Councillor and he it was who built the Victoria Hall in Crawley, opened in 1920 on a site a few yards north of the former Rising Sun Inn (see 4). A generation who danced and were entertained there had cause to be grateful to him. The shop on the right of this picture was demolished in 1958.

52. *Bartley and Ward's, Crawley (1920's)*. Just off the High Street, where it turned into Three Bridges Road, lay the industrious concern of Bartley and Ward, established c1899 when two young men left the employment of James Longley & Sons and took over the Crawley building firm run by the Gates family since 1855. Tommy Bartley and John Ward made their first major contribution to local life with the installation of the new clock on St. John's Church in 1901, but the firm also had a hand in the building of Station Road, where Bartley, his mother, John Ward and John Ward senior all lived – in four separate houses! By 1913 plumbing, house decorating and funeral work had all been added to the repertoire – and with two yards at its disposal (one in Cross Keys, the other in Three Bridges Road) it ultimately attracted a take-over bid! This was successful and in 1930 new owners Hall, Beddel & Co began using their Crawley branch to provide joinery for their contracts in London.

53. *Bartley and Ward's, Crawley (detail)*. There were 16 to 20 men in the firm's workshop on the first floor, where carpentry and funeral work mixed cosily together and the noise of the buzz-saw droned a familiar tune to passers by. What a tale these chaps could tell I'm sure... Of the time they carved a funeral stone for Lady Longley's mother perhaps, which carried the immortal message: 'Praise The Lord, Bartley and Ward!' Or the occasion when Tommy's daughter-in-law was expecting a child at her home opposite St. John's Church – and the bellringers were oblivious to all entreaties to 'Stop that infernal noise', having thoughtfully locked themselves in the tower... In 1957 the business moved to new premises at 58 Haslett Avenue and the old home was demolished. A second take-over in 1969 resulted in the closure of all but the funeral business, and this has since removed to a former school and tea house close to St. John's Church, bearing the appropriate name 'Gravesend Cottage'.

54. *High Street, Crawley (c1913).* Moving back into the High Street we find a row of shops that were tacked onto the front of some handsome Victorian villas around 1905. The conversion was not unpleasant though and the addition of a wrought iron balcony gave a distinct touch of elegance. Mr. Wilkins, who ran the butcher's shop in a prime position on the corner, also found time to act as both Parish Councillor and churchwarden. Indeed, in the latter capacity local amusement was derived from the sight of Mr. Wilkins and Mr. Conlan (from North House School) processing down the aisle of St. John's Church in brotherly duty on a Sunday morning, even though it was widely known that the schoolmaster was heavily behind on his butcher's bills! Before being fronted by a shop incidentally this particular villa provided Crawley's first banking service (see 56). Next to Wilkin's was a sweet shop run by Mr. Brooks and stocked from his own sweet factory just off Springfield Road.

55. *Crawley Peace Celebrations (1919)*. People *loved* marching through Crawley – whether they were bandsmen, London to Brighton walkers, fund raisers, protestors, carnival participants, members of memorial processions, or, as here, swelling a good turnout to celebrate the conclusion of the First World War. Predictably the festivities included athletic events! This is the same stretch of road as in the previous photo, though with all the flags and bunting you'd hardly recognise it! Incidentally, compare this photo with plate 46. Apart from the activity you'll notice that the shop fronts in the middle of the 1905 picture have now been pushed forward to match those of Messrs Wilkins, Brooks and Stokes. The premises of Titcomb's the auctioneers are on the right.

56. *Crawley High Street (about 1906)*. This is the view enjoyed by those near the head of the procession on the previous page. Titcomb's, the auctioneers and estate agents, are on the immediate left, with Willett's, the printers, in the tall building just beyond. The bizarre edifice on the right belongs to the London, County and Westminster Bank, the first permanent bank in Crawley. Its hours were from 10 to 4 during the week and from 10 till 1 on Saturdays. The Capital and Counties Bank was the first to provide a service in Crawley though, two of their gentlemen popping over from Horsham in a pony and trap on Tuesdays, Fridays and Fair Days, in late Victorian times. They opened for three hours per day at the villa on the corner of Three Bridges Road (which subsequently became Wilkins' the butcher's shop), before acquiring their first permanent premises in 1902 – in the Brighton Road, next to the signal box.

57. *Memorial procession for King Edward VIIth (May 1910)*. The king died on 6th May and his reputation as a roué did nothing to diminish the affection in which he was held throughout the country. Crawley's procession was on its way to Lower Square, at the other end of the village, where the memorial service was to be held. This photo was taken just at the other side of Titcomb's – and probably by the firm of Willett, whose shop is clearly shown and who produced some excellent photographic postcards of the village. Crawley Temperance Society, whose banner featured prominently in so many local processions, came into being in the mid-1880's, the Reverend J. McAuslane, the Baptist Minister, being the instigator. It is said that when he first arrived in Crawley he persuaded 200 people to sign the pledge in the space of three nights!

58. *The New Post Office (c1933).* The first Post Office in Crawley appeared in 1802, occupying a front room at the White Hart, where the proprietor, James Swift, doubled as postmaster. At that time Crawley was one of the three main post offices on the Brighton coaching run, the others being at Sutton and Cuckfield. Night mail coaches added to the volume of traffic when they were introduced in 1812. Swift's nephew, William Mitchell, followed him as postmaster and, around 1840, transferred the business to his own newly erected home just north of the inn. After a brief move to a house next to Vine Cottage (c1882) the Post Office then acquired custom-built premises complete with sorting office in New Road (later Robinson Road) in 1895. (A decision to close by 9 pm each night and to take a half-holiday every week was greeted with outrage, however!) Finally, in 1928, the Post Office moved into this High Street showpiece, Titcomb's the auctioneers having been demolished to make way for it.

59. *High Street, Crawley (c1930)*. This picture was taken a few years before the Second World War, in which both the new Post Office and Willett's were heavily damaged in an air raid (February 1943). Both were rebuilt, and the Post Office eventually moved to its present site in the Boulevard in 1959. Willett's were responsible for printing the Crawley Observer for many years by the way – founded as 'Simmins's Weekly Advertiser' in 1881, changing to the 'Sussex and Surrey Courier' almost immediately, and only acquiring its present title in July 1946. The bus belongs to the East Surrey Traction Company and is on its way from West Croydon to Handcross. The Company was based in Reigate and its open topped buses first reached Crawley in February 1916. Between 1922 and 1929 vehicles were kept overnight at the White Hart (a throwback to the coaching age!), but in June 1929 the Company opened a bus garage in Crawley. East Surrey became part of London Transport in 1933.

60. *Upper High Street, looking north (c1900).* We have now reached the southern end of the High Street and, if we look back towards Crawley, we see the view as it was at the end of Victoria's reign. This is the earliest postcard that I know of showing Crawley, stamped 1902, but almost certainly taken a year or two earlier, and still showing trees outside the chemist's shop. In the 1850's there was a sawpit on this site and when John Leach first occupied his new shop c1862 he was billed both as chemist and dentist! He dropped the dentistry in the mid-1880's it would seem, but then acted as agent for a wine and spirit merchant from 1878 to 1899. If you think that combination of activities is unusual then look at the shop on the immediate left, owned briefly by W.W. Bannister, West Green engineers. They not only looked after cars (and this must be one of the earliest 'petrol stations' in the country) but were soon to run a photographic shop in the Brighton Road as well!

61. *Upper High Street, looking north (c1908).* Around 1904 John Leach was succeeded as chemist by Edward Brooke, the trees were swept away, and the shop front modernised. The trade was as bizarre as ever though, Brooke advertising that he was a 'Dealer in Horse and Cattle Medicines' as well as the more conventional human remedies. The whole of this end of the street dates from the latter half of the 19th century of course, when the railway arrived, and prior to that the High Street ended with Mark Lemon's house, Vine Cottage, clearly visible just beyond the architectural oddity of a bank on the left! (See 41 and 56.) This is a fine view of the street taken from the Railway Hotel balcony by Percival Snelling, a local photographer and printer, who seemed to go to some trouble to capture the people and the 'feel' of the village!

62. *Brighton Road and level crossing, Crawley (c1916).* 'Modern Crawley is disfigured by the abomination of a busy railway level-crossing that bars the main road and causes an immeasurable flow of bad language. It affords a very good idea of the delays and annoyances at the old turnpike-gates, without their excuse for existence.' Thus wrote Charles Harper in 1906, at a time when the 'motor car' was still a relatively new sight on English roads. By the 1920's and 1930's, however, the trickle had turned into a cascade, especially on summer weekends, and the 'tailback' when the crossing gates clanged shut had to be seen to be believed. Action was clearly necessary and the opening of Crawley By Pass in 1939 came not a moment too soon. When this picture was taken though, c1916, it was still possible for ladies to saunter down the middle of the street wheeling their bicycles!

63. *Crawley railway station (about 1882).* The railway from London to Brighton reached Three Bridges in July 1841, and it was not long before serious consideration was given to branch lines serving East Grinstead and Horsham. Two routes to Horsham were mooted. The first would leave the main line a little south of Balcombe and reach Horsham via the Ouse valley. The second would veer west at Three Bridges and arrive at the market town via Crawley and Faygate. The Act of Parliament passed on 21st July 1845 opted for the 'Crawley' route, and the 8½ mile line, complete with 18 bridges and 8 level crossings, opened on 14th February 1848. Crawley's new railway station adjoined the level crossing and Brighton Road, and by 1853 there were 6 trains a day stopping in the village, and a staff of 8 to look after them. This number seems to have doubled by 1882, but at least one of those in the picture has wandered over from the nearby flour mill! The line was extended to Petworth in 1859 by the way.

64. *Brighton Road, Crawley (c1909).* In the 1850's, soon after the railway was built and the station opened, a hotel called the Station Inn was constructed on the Brighton Road, next to the Horsham bound platform. (On the left of plate 62 and on extreme left here.) This rapidly became one of the village's chief meeting places and centres of entertainment and it was here in the 1860's that Mark Lemon could be found, rubbing shoulders with other local luminaries. In later Victorian times it was renamed The Railway Hotel and is currently known as 'The Rocket'. The station itself was demolished in 1968 and replaced by a new one 300 yards to the east, but the signal box is still there, having only retired from active service in 1986. The grandiose building behind it belonged to the London and County Bank, and was erected in 1901 on a site previously occupied by Fillery and Nightingale, the corn & coal merchants. It was eventually taken over by Lloyds Bank.

65. *Rolls Royce accident, Crawley (1920's)*. Whenever the level crossing gates were closed pedestrians were able to cross from one side of the railway line to the other by means of a short subway, which ran between the western gate and the signal box. It was a small, dank, unattractive passage, and is the sort of memory of one's home town that stays in the mind long after more pleasant and more important memories recede. Of all those who have descended to its lower depths though, none can have been more unexpected or more unwelcome than this visitor! If you look at the previous picture you'll see that it can't have been easy to make such an error of judgement! The subway disappeared in 1978 by the way when continental gates were installed.

66. *Brighton Road, Crawley, looking north (c1903).* South of the level crossing the main street is known as 'The Brighton Road', with the Station Inn (as it used to be called) at its threshold. There weren't any shops next to the Inn in the mid-19th century of course, only a garden and lawn, and in the later Victorian years it ran an extensive livery business, hiring out horses to travellers in the days before the motor car. Station Inn Yard also contained a printing business run by Samuel Simmins (which subsequently transferred to the High Street), and next door there was a large flour mill run by his father William. (Brother George founded the local paper, now familiar as the Crawley Observer.) The small row of shops stretching from the Railway Hotel to East Park was a late 19th century addition and up to 1905 was known as Station Terrace. This photo was probably taken for the benefit of Miss Newbery (shop on right), who sold postcards as well as needlework.

67. *Brighton Road, west side (c1923).* A photo taken from this spot in 1840 would have shown almost nothing but trees and fields stretching all the way to Vine Cottage in the distance. What a transformation in just eighty years! Apart from the Station Inn I believe that the earliest 'settlers' on this side of the tracks were the occupants of the broom yard headed by Thomas Biggs. By 1874 they had been joined by the Ockenden family, who started a brewery just off Springfield Road, and in 1882 Nightingale & Fillery opened their corn merchant's on the corner facing the signal box. Crawley's second garage, seen on the left, was founded by 'Gaddy' Gadson c1905, and he it was who also took over the adjoining cinema around 1913. After the First World War there used to be an auction room at the Tin Hut in East Park by the way, and the chaps with hand carts are almost certainly taking their winning lots home! Just look at the flappers in their cloche hats too!

68. *The Imperial Picture Theatre, Crawley (c1911)*. Crawley's first cinema – known as the 'Tin Hut' – was sited in East Park, some 200 yards from this scene. It not only had wooden benches for seats but was so small that the projectionist had to reach his box by means of an outside staircase. In 1911, however, a Mr. H.W. Hire opened the newly constructed 'Imperial Picture Theatre' in the Brighton Road, and the 'Tin Hut', shorn of custom, was quickly reduced to the status of a roller skating rink. At the time this picture was taken the Imperial's programme – seven silent 'shorts' accompanied by 'Mr. Syd Raymond's Songs' – was probably typical of picture palace fare throughout the country. The success of the new venture naturally attracted attention and, in 1913, the Imperial was taken over by Mr. C. Gadson, one of Crawley's most go-ahead businessmen, who had owned the garage and 'motor-agents' next door since 1905.

69. *The Imperial Cinema (c1922).* During the 26 years that Mr. Gadson ran the cinema it was used not merely for showing films but also as a meeting place. Prime Minister Ramsay MacDonald made a speech here in October 1933 for instance, warning Hitler's Germany of the consequences of leaving the international disarmament conference. Both the British Legion and the League of Nations Union used it regularly – and it was a familiar venue for popular charity concerts. It was also a backdrop for the many marches and parades that took place up and down the main street in the first 25 years of the century, mostly in aid of creating funds for the local hospital. Primarily though, it was the focus for escapist entertainment on the 'silver screen', 'Free Air', the feature on show here, being the tale of a banker's daughter who falls for a small town garage owner. Just the ticket for a cinema conveniently sited next door to a garage and a bank.

70. *Crawley Cinema fire (1928)*. The cinema was originally constructed without a balcony, but ironically, on 4th August 1928, soon after one was added, the building was completely gutted by fire. Fortunately for local film fans it was quickly rebuilt, and reopened for business in July 1929, with a smart new front, a foyer tiled in blue and grey, seating for 664, and an orchestra of four to provide the music. 'The talkies' arrived almost immediately!… In 1938, however, a new cinema, 'The Embassy', opened on the site of the former Albany Temperance Hotel, and within a year had succeeded in capturing most of the Imperial's custom, mainly by virtue of its more central position. With the approach of war closure was inevitable and, in April 1939, the old cinema faded to black for the last time. After a spell as an auction room in the 1940's and 1950's it finally became part of the adjoining 'motor show rooms' where its remains now rest.

71. *Longley's Fire (March 1924).* The disaster at the Imperial Picture Theatre was Crawley's second major fire of the twentieth century. Ironically the first occurred only a short distance away when the joinery works of James Longley and Sons exploded into flames early in the morning of 20th March 1924. It seems that sparks from a passing railway engine set fire to a pile of leaves, and these in turn fired one of Longley's workshops adjoining the line. A strong wind was blowing, the yard was full of inflammable builders' materials, and in no time the whole concern was ablaze. Both Crawley and Horsham Fire Brigades were summoned and the fire was so fierce that, at its height, falling particles set light to Doctor Matthew's house, 400 yards away in the Brighton Road. Within four hours every building on the premises had been gutted, sixty machines were destroyed and the entire stock was wiped out. It was a calamity that almost ruined what was to become Crawley's most famous business.

72. *Brighton Road, Crawley, looking north (1903).* Returning to the Brighton Road from Longley's premises in East Park (the road seen on the right), this is a picture of the southern end of the main street shortly after the final row of shops was completed. The first shop on this side of East Park was the corn and coal merchants business run by Moses Nightingale, previously occupying the site opposite the signal box and removed to its new location c1899. In that year there were no houses between the shop and Nightingale's home, Hazeldene, 100 yards to the right. Bannister's, who were engineers and machinists, had a works in West Green and ran a shop just north of the level crossing (see 60) before arriving here c1901. They not only sold motor cars and agricultural machinery, hired out bicycles and supplied 'electric lighting' but also ran what must have been the earliest photographic shop in the village too! The gap on the left is where the cinema was built in 1911 by the way.

Brighton Road, Crawley,
in February 1907.

73. *Brighton Road, Crawley (February 1907).* Beyond the cinema and new shops, spreading confidently along the Brighton Road, lay another area, which Charles Harper eloquently described in 1906 as 'the Park Lane or Belgravia of Crawley – the residential and superior modern district of country houses, each in midst of its own little pleasance'. It was a boulevard of solicitors, auctioneers, doctors, clergy, military men, men of wealth, those 'who had arrived'. Some of the names tell their own story in 1907: Coole and Haddock (solicitors), Wood, Son and Gardner (auctioneers), Dr. Percival Wood, Dr. Sidney Matthews J.P., Lieutenant Hall R.N., Moses Nightingale, Dr. Timothy Martin J.P., the Reverend Charles Beresford Knox, Harold Robert Yerburgh-Bonsey... Incidentally, this photograph, by Belchamber and Son, also of the Brighton Road, is one of a series of Crawley in the snow, the only known examples of the firm's work.

The Half Moon · Hotel, Hoggs Hill, Crawley.

74. *The Half Moon Hotel, Hoggs Hill, Crawley (c1905)*. 'Nearing Crawley a wag enquires whether we are aware that this is the longest village in the world, and on admitting our ignorance of this geographical fact, he points out the 'Sun' at one end and the 'Moon' at the other.' Thus Charles Harper recorded the classic local joke in 1892 as he traversed what was actually over a mile from the Sun Inn to the 'Half Moon', reached at the top of an incline just south of Crawley, known by the engagingly rural name, Hogs Hill. It was a title which probably originated from the personal name 'Willmo Le Hog' recorded in the Subsidy Rolls of 1327. Old Hogshill Farm, close to the beerhouse, may have existed in the 16th century. The inn itself is only documented on a map of 1872 however, and was rather curiously rebuilt in 1890, perhaps to bring it closer to an improved road slicing through the top of the hill. At any rate the new inn cost £594, and an East Grinstead man called Pledge built it.

75. *The Water Tower, Crawley (c1906)*. The arrival of the railway encouraged new settlement, particularly in the period from 1860 onwards. New houses brought problems however, water and sanitation amongst them, and in the 1880's sewage was still discharged untreated into local brooks and ditches. A clean water supply was therefore fraught with difficulty. When Alice Longley, wife of Charles Longley the builder, died of diptheria in 1897, matters came to a head and a sense of shock, represented in a funeral procession 300 yards long, was followed by determination to put matters right. A syndicate was set up, a test bore was struck, and good clean water was eventually discovered 960 feet below the surface here at Goffs Park, close to Longley's family home of Rathcote. A company was formed (Crawley & District Water Company led by Charles and James Longley, Doctor Martin and Moses Nightingale), and by 1898 clean water was being supplied to many parts of Crawley.

76. *The Elms (c1913)*. This elegant house was situated in the Old Horsham Road on the south-western outskirts of Crawley, and in later, humbler years, was known as Buckswood Grange. In its heyday, however, it was titled 'The Elms', and positively exuded wealth. Back in 1859 for example the owner was the Hon. Fanny Charlotte Montgomery, third child of the first Baron Leconfield, who was not only a staunch Roman Catholic but who also possessed a villa in Naples. Realising that Crawley had had no Roman Catholic church since the time of the Reformation she invited a group of Italian Franciscans to establish a mission here – and this they did, using a coach shed in the grounds of the Elms as a temporary church. (See also 92-94.) Another distinguished owner was Leslie Stuart, composer of 'Mighty Mother England' and other patriotic songs. In later life the house was used as a girls' school, a residence for homeless families, and a Civil Defence Centre, before being demolished in the 1950's.

77. *A pretty fete in the grounds of The Elms, Crawley (1908).* By 1908 The Elms had become the property of Mrs. John Goddard (Secretary and Treasurer of the Crawley and Worth Primrose League), and in that year a memorable event took place in the grounds. The occasion was the visit to Crawley of Her Royal Highness Princess Alexander of Teck, in aid of funds for the newly enlarged Cottage Hospital in Post Office Road. A 'Grand Bazaar and Fete' was arranged at The Elms, and on the appointed day, 1st July 1908, Princess Alexander duly arrived and spent the best part of the afternoon there, much to the delight of local 'society'. The event was well covered by local photographers, as well as the national press – and the following series of photographs capture the mood of a delightful afternoon at the height of Edwardian England.

78. *'At the Bazaar' (1908).* The setting for the event could hardly have been bettered as The Elms possessed the finest gardens in the district, sweeping down to a lake which lay on the far side of the present by-pass. The Princess dutifully visited all the stalls, including the 'Garden Stall', seen on the right here, and run by Lady Luscombe and Mrs. Percival Wood, though it is doubtful whether those two good ladies managed to persuade their royal visitor to take a garden roller home with her! The gentlemen, with their waistcoats, boaters and moustaches – and the ladies, with their flowered hats, long skirts and parasols, seem the epitome of Edwardian elegance. The only discordant note is struck by the chap in the middle, who is clutching a pipe and clearly wondering whether it is correct etiquette to smoke in the presence of royalty – or whether he should tactfully slide behind a nearby bush!

THE PRINCESS VISITING THE STALLS

79. *The Princess visiting The Stalls (1908)*. Princess Alexander was a grandchild of Queen Victoria and eldest daughter of Prince Leopold, Victoria's third son. Her real name was Alice, but on her marriage to Prince Alexander of Teck, younger brother of the future Queen Mary, she became known as Princess Alexander. She was born in 1884, so she would have been about 24 at the time of her visit to Crawley. Following the war she and her husband became Earl and Countess of Athlone, and, after a spell in Canada, the couple renewed their association with the Crawley area, settling at Brantridge Park, not far from Rowfant. The Princess came to Crawley once again in November 1939, this time to present the prizes at Milton Mount College, the large girls' school near Ridley's Corner. When she eventually died in 1982, Princess Alice, Countess of Athlone, was the oldest surviving member of the Royal Family.

80. *Mrs. Goddard (on the left) sells pottery to the Princess (1908).* The stallholders at the Royal Fete were all apparently female – and read like a 'Who's Who' of Crawley society at the time. Apart from Mrs. Goddard herself there were Mrs. Barrett-Lennard the Rector's wife, Mrs. McAuslane the Baptist Minister's wife, Mrs. Martin the doctor's wife, the Mrs. Longley, Nightingale and Penfold, wives of prominent Crawley businessmen – and no less than six members of the Nix family who owned the Tilgate Park Estate. A list of stalls is revealing too; – Plain and Fancy Needlework, Pottery and Dolls, Sweets, Garden, Provisions, Parcels and Packing (!), no less than four 'Fancy' stalls – and one enigmatically labelled 'Coal Scuttle'! (The mind boggles!) After taking tea with Mrs. Goddard in the drawing room the Princess departed for Crawley & Ifield Cottage Hospital at 4.30 p.m., in the company of Doctor Martin, the senior Crawley doctor.

81. *Visit of HRH Princess Alexander of Teck to Crawley (1908)*. The Princess had travelled down from London by car, which was still something of a novelty as far as royalty were concerned. Indeed, as you can see, the horse and carriage had by no means been superseded at this date! It will also be apparent that the whole community had turned out to greet its royal visitor, none being more enthusiastic than the residents of Three Bridges, where the Princess had originally been due to arrive by train. As the local paper put it *Hearing that the people at Three Bridges had effected certain decorations in view of her passage through the village, Her Royal Highness very thoughtfully altered her course at Horley… in order to enter Crawley via Three Bridges and so save the inhabitants at the latter place any feeling of disappointment.* Her journey to the hospital, late in the afternoon, was an equal attraction.

82. *Cottage Hospital, Crawley (c1907).* Up to late Victorian times Crawley only had one doctor's practice, covering an extremely wide area and with the doctor doubling as local dentist. John Dungate was chief practitioner from about 1780 to 1798, Robert Smith from 1799 to 1828, Thomas Smith from 1828 to 1862 and Timothy Martin from 1862 onwards. Following the establishment of Crawley and Ifield parish councils a Cottage Hospital was created in Post Office Road (see 83) in 1896, funded by the public and redeploying a girls' home erected by Sarah Robinson. It proved its mettle during the Handcross Accident of 1906 when the hospital's ambulances transported several of the 24 injured there. It was then enlarged to provide nine beds and one cot and the visiting Princess told the Matron, Miss Davison, that it was 'equal to, though naturally smaller than a London Hospital'. In 1939 work began on a new hospital in West Green and patients were soon transferred there. The old building now belongs to a local solicitor.

83. *Post Office Road (1907)*. The road containing the hospital did not exist until the 1850's, and Sarah Robinson's British School, established by 1854, was possibly its first building. A Bethel Chapel was founded here in 1858 and the road probably got its original name, Church Road, when a second church, the Trinity Congregational one, was established in 1863. By the time George Ockenden opened a brewery next door to the school in the 1870's the combination of God, education and alcohol must have struck the authorities as incongruous, and so the street was retitled New Road. Then, in 1905, ten years after Charles Mitchell built his Post Office (seen on the right), it became known as Post Office Road. Finally, in 1939 the name was changed yet again, to Robinson Road, though the Post Office had moved eleven years earlier, the delay occurring because a local trader had to use up a large stack of headed notepaper! The Sussex saying 'We won't be druv' was never more appropriate!

84. *West Green, Crawley (c1911)*. On the route leading west from Crawley to Ifield lies a district first referred to as West Green c1532. Two of the oldest cottages here date back to the 16th century too, but when the tithe map was drawn up in 1841 there were still no more than twenty dwellings in this vicinity. The Crown Inn (on the left, looking towards Crawley) was originally just a cottage, surrounded by an orchard, but seems to have become a beerhouse by 1890. St. John's Road, just beyond, is a remnant of Small's Lane, the routeway to Horsham prior to the mid-18th century (see 32). The shop on the right belonged to John Till, a baker, who sold bread and cakes in an extension to his front room. The bakehouse was at the rear, and everyone who had a Christmas turkey or birthday cake too large to go in their own oven brought it there to be cooked – for a small fee. Behind the shops, which are still there, lay the largest of Crawley's two broom yards.

85. *West Green Church of England School.* In 1831 a school was founded in Ifield Road, West Green, just 200 yards from Crawley High Street. Mrs. Sarah Robinson, from Manor Farm, raised the funds to build it, and though she was a staunch Quaker it was designed to be entirely non-denominational. John Mason Neale, the famous hymnwriter, visited it in 1842, whilst occupying the living at Crawley for six weeks, and told his fiancee: *I never saw cleaner rooms or more airy, or cleaner children. They have but two teachers for the boys – poor men, not knowing very much, but very civil – and one for the girls; there are 35 of the latter and 70 of the former.* Shortly afterwards the school was restricted to children of parents attending the Anglican church and it became known as the National or Church of England School. Apart from being hit by a bomb in 1943 it led an uneventful life and was eventually closed in 1955, pupils being transferred to a new school in Ifield.

86. *West Green, Crawley, St. Peter's Church (1905)*. **Facing the Crown is St. Peter's Church, supported in the background by a public house, now known as The Swan but originally the site of The Bricklayers Arms. Built c1855 the latter served as a monument to those who created a range of new streets and houses here, especially in the last quarter of the 19th century. Chief amongst these were members of the Ockenden family, who constructed St. Peter's, St. John's, Spencer's and Victoria and built a Mission Church called St. Mary Magdalene's, opened in 1880 as a chapel of ease to Ifield Parish Church. Within twelve years however, its 240 seats were viewed as inadequate, and this church, St. Peter's, was built nearby as a replacement. It cost £2,800, held 439 people and was opened in 1893. West Green finally became a separate ecclesiastical parish in 1901... Acid-bath murderer John George Haigh disposed of his unfortunate victims in Leopold Road during 1948 and 1949 by the way, just 300 yards west of the church.**

87. *Crawley from the air, looking north (1929)*. Crawley's pattern of development occurred in three stages. After the church was established in the mid-13th century (top right) a number of large timber-framed dwellings and farmhouses spread northwards along the main street over the next 450 years. These included The Ancient Priors, Punch Bowl, The Tree and The George. Then from 1700 to 1840 the highway was gradually improved, coach traffic was introduced, and turnpike roads came into existence. This was the period when the George Annexe arose in the middle of the street, and the White Hart and Miller's saddlery were established, all related to the new found trade. Finally, after the railway exploded across the middle of the picture in 1848, new houses followed in West Green (top left), Springfield and Perryfield Roads (bottom left), and East Park and Malthouse Road (bottom right). At the same time new shops were created running southwards from the Square and over the level crossing into the Brighton Road.

SPRINGFIELD ROAD, CRAWLEY.

103749 A. E. Willett, Printer & Stationer, Crawley.

88. *Springfield Road, Crawley (c1906).* South of the railway line and west of the Brighton Road lay an area called 'New Town', the first to be developed in Crawley following the arrival of the railway in 1848. Most of the construction appears to have taken place in the 1870's and 1880's and the new local paper, Simmins's Weekly Advertiser, talks of 'the many cottages recently erected at West Green and in New Town' in its fourth issue of 13th April 1881. Springfield Road, seen here, was next to the railway line and was built by Richard Cook & Sons, along with Perryfield Road and West Street. The name 'Springfield' derived from the area around Goffs Hill, where Captain (later Lord) de Blaquiere was living at Springfields House by 1870. By 1890 Springfield Road contained a brewery, a commercial school and a broom yard, with a laundry and boot maker's close by. The footpath on the left is interesting too since Southern Railways had to close it once a year to retain ownership!

MALTHOUSE ROAD, CRAWLEY.

103743   A. E. Willett, Printer & Stationer, Crawley

89. *Malthouse Road (c1905).* In October 1881 the firm of James Longley and Sons took over the brickyard and railway siding south-east of Crawley previously owned by William Sumner. Surprisingly, brickmaking was discontinued almost at once, but having set up a works, brought joinery equipment from his former premises at Turners Hill, and built himself a house, James Longley gradually began to purchase the land around him. Malthouse Road was the first to draw his attention, and although a few houses already existed there, Longleys quickly added 18 semi-detached cottages for the benefit of their workforce, completing them by 1882. Other cottages and villas followed, including ten in East Park, and by 1909 the firm owned 63 properties with a total rateable value of £1,718, making Mr. Longley quite the biggest houseowner in the village. Despite the new dwellings, however, Crawley was still a rural settlement at heart, as you can see from the man carrying a pole of rabbits on his shoulder!

90. *Baptist Chapel, Station Road (1905).* Heading north over the level crossing, and turning right at the chemist's shop you came to Station Road, the Baptist Chapel, and a strange segment of Crawley history! In 1882 a fiery 23 year old Scots preacher called James McAuslane steamed into the awakening village and, backed by Charles Warren the plumber and William Hewett the stationmaster, founded a lively Temperance Movement. The people of Crawley were so impressed that they invited James to become the pastor of the local Congregational Church, but legal difficulties barred the way, and a group of sixty 'seceders' broke away with McAuslane at their head. Within seven months they had purchased this site for £110, and in November 1883 work started on the new Baptist Chapel. It cost £565 to build, held 375 people and served the faithful well until devastated by German bombs in February 1943. Though patched up and serving as the public library from 1953 to 1960 it was eventually demolished in 1983.

91. *Station Road (1907)*. Round the corner from the Baptist Chapel was the northern half of Station Road, with St. John's Church and Gravesend Cottage (see 53) blocking the view. In the mid-19th century there were an orchard and a field on the left, but by late Victorian times these had been replaced by a row of houses built by Harry Osbourn, who lived in the one nearest to the Baptist Chapel. The oldest houses in the road were the four at the far end on the right, but in 1884 they were joined by Crawley's first police station, constructed by Richard Cook and Sons. The last house to be erected was put up in 1903, probably by Bartley and Ward, there being two Bartleys and two Wards living in the street in 1904. William Hewett the station master also lived here and when he retired from the railway he ran a coal office by the station entrance. (You can see him on the far right of 63.) All the old houses in Station Road were demolished in 1985.

92. *Crawley Church, Three Bridges Road (c1907).* The road from Crawley to Three Bridges was something of a watershed in local life since the two primary churches in the village faced each other across it, Anglican on the right, Roman Catholic, just behind the trees, on the left. St. John's Church, the Anglican one, had of course been Catholic too when first founded in the 13th century. After the Reformation though local Roman Catholics were left with no place in which to worship for nearly 300 years, and it was only in 1859 that the owner of 'The Elms', Mrs. Montgomery, invited a group of Italian Franciscans to form a Roman Catholic Church once again in the village. (See 76.) Initially they used a converted coach shed in the grounds of 'The Elms' as a temporary church, but in 1860 a generous benefactor appeared in the shape of Mrs. Montgomery's wealthy cousin, Francis Blunt of Crabbet Park.

93. *Franciscan Monastery, Crawley.* Francis Blunt set about building a new and permanent Catholic Church in Crawley and, in return for a token payment of 10 shillings, gave the friars 'All that piece or parcel of land situate in the Parish of Ifield... containing five acres and three roods or thereabouts being portion of a farm belonging to the said Francis Scawen Blunt known as the Old White Hart Farm... Together with the Church and Presbytery'. He also undertook to pay the friars £100 a year towards their costs and, in return, the priests agreed to say Mass three times a week in the chapel at Crabbet Park. The new church was duly opened by Thomas Grant, Bishop of Southwark, on 12th October 1861. The foundations had been poorly laid however, without concrete footings and utilising Crabbet stone that had not been allowed to season, and in consequence everyone was relieved when the Presbytery was erected (right), thereby preventing the church from toppling over.

94. *Franciscan Monastery, Crawley, The High Altar.* Blunt died in 1872, at only 33 years of age, and was laid to rest in the 'Blunt Chapel', below a full length alabaster likeness created by his brother Wilfred. Then, when Mrs. Montgomery died in 1893, she bequeathed a small marble and alabaster side-altar to the church, from her villa in Italy. It was accompanied by a portrait of St. Anthony of Padua, and this inspired the creation of a 'Guild of St. Anthony' in 1895, whose membership soared world-wide over the next fifty years. Indeed it was so successful that in 1946 Pope Pius XIIth permitted the church to be renamed 'The Church of St. Francis and St. Anthony'. (You can see St. Francis over the main altar.) With the growth of the post-war New Town however, 'Blunt's church' was no longer of adequate size and a new church was opened in 1959, the old premises being gradually demolished... Even the friars left in the end, rising costs forcing them to hand over to secular priests in 1980.

95. *Crawley, Three Bridges Road (1907).* Emerging from the Franciscan Friary and looking towards Three Bridges this was the rural view that greeted the local man in 1907, there being almost no settlement between Crawley and its neighbouring village up to that time. A small Catholic school made its appearance here in 1938 however, sited just behind the trees on the left, and built at a cost of £5,000. It had wooden classrooms and I particularly remember it because I attended for two years from 1948 to 1950 and got into a fight on my first morning! The local recreation ground, known to everyone as the 'rec', lay just beyond. This was opened after the First World War and the equipment in it was donated by Moses and Ruth Nightingale during the 1920's. A film taken at the official opening in May 1929 shows amazing scenes of grown adults swarming over the roundabouts! Though part of the 'rec' still exists the area on the left is now the site of the New Town shopping centre!

96. *The Plough, Three Bridges (c1902).* Three Bridges lies a mile to the east of Crawley and is now a part of the New Town. In Victorian times, however, it was a separate 'railway village', owing its growth to the arrival of the Brighton line in 1841. Nevertheless there was a tiny hamlet before 'the iron horse' passed through, and the Plough Inn (on the left) was at its centre, being clearly marked on the tithe map of 1840, with just two or three houses and a shop around it . In the Victorian and Edwardian era visiting organ grinders were frequently seen outside the Inn, and these were joined, twice a year, by a 'week-end fair', which pulled in on the minute village green just to the right of the photo. Perhaps it was as well that the fair was only a small-scale event where everything was hand-powered, including the roundabouts! The shop on the right was owned by Tryaton Nathaniel Randall and his two daughters incidentally, and was a mainstay of village life for many years.

Three Bridges.

97. *Hedley House, Three Bridges (1905).* A little further down the street and looking back towards Crawley, the horse has pulled up outside Hedley House, owned by local tailor James Mowl. Mowl was also superintendent of Three Bridges Mission Hall, the first church in Three Bridges and located in New Street, just behind his house. He commenced services there in 1876, after holding them in his own home for a year. He had two daughters, Eliza and Maria, and they ran a small private school for infants and girls in a building next door to the Hall. This school, latterly based at Hedley House, continued until the 1930's. The building with the peaked gable just behind the cart was one rented as a residence to members of the local police force. Opposite Hedley House was one of the entrance lodges to Tilgate Estate, seat of the Nix family, and occupying vast acres stretching all the way to the Parish Lane at Peas Pottage.

98. *Three Bridges High Street, looking east (c1904)*. The name 'Three Bridges' originated in the 16th century but no one knows whether the bridges referred to lay on the track from Crawley to Worth, or the route from North Road to Tinsley Green and Charlwood. Moreover the two roads and the embryo settlement itself only appear on a map for the first time in 1795, though they *are* accompanied by Crosskeys Farm and Hazlewick Mill and the Mill is recorded as existing in 1622. What *is* certain is that after the railway arrived a whole string of new roads and houses began to appear, mostly constructed for the growing number of railway employees, and New Street (seen on the left) was the first. It was created in the 1860's and by 1895 it not only contained the Mission Hall and private school previously described, but also a local photographer, J.W. Slator, who subsequently occupied a glass roofed studio opposite North Road at the eastern end of the High Street.

Three Bridges, Post Office.

99. *Three Bridges Post Office (1906).* Just beyond the horse and cart in the centre of the previous photograph lay London House, now the site of a major roundabout. In those days however, it was home to Three Bridges Sub-Post Office, which had been established sometime between 1866 and 1878 with a Mr. Isaac Ellis in charge. Joseph Spencer Brown took over in Edwardian times and by 1916 he could boast of three deliveries at 7.00a.m., 10.30a.m. and 6.30p.m. every day, with one on Sunday mornings – at 7.00 a.m.! (So much for the advances of mechanisation and post codes!) The Post Office also doubled as a draper's and general store (a real 'corner shop' in every sense!) and its 'flood sales', held whenever the nearby River Mole burst its banks (which it did quite regularly), were justly famous!...In the 1920's Lloyd's Bank took over the house on the left to provide a twice weekly banking service to the expanding community, and though it wouldn't pass muster as prestige premises today, nobody seemed to mind too much at the time!

100. *Three Bridges High Street, looking west (c1904).* Looking back towards Crawley from the Post Office this view eloquently demonstrates the unsophisticated nature of the village in Edwardian times. The left hand side of the road consisted of fields and trees and marked the northern boundary of the Tilgate Estate. The only building in view on that side, now familiar as Barclays Bank, was nothing more than a humble entrance lodge in those days... And look at the state of the road, evidence indeed that this was still a rural community, with farmers herding cattle and carting produce to Crawley's regular markets and twice-yearly Fairs! The writer of this postcard certainly had tongue in cheek when noting that: 'This is the city where we alight when coming to Woolborough!'

101. *Butchers's Cart, Three Bridges*. They don't deliver like this any more, do they? This immaculate cart belonged to Snelling's, a family firm who owned a shop on the High Street between the Plough and Locomotive Inns. They appear to have been in business locally by 1866, and by 1895 George Snelling, the second generation, was advertising the delights of 'Home Made Sausages and Prime Pickled Tongues'; 'Corned Beef' being added to the repertoire by the time of the First World War. Mr. Snelling lived at Lime Tree House, Pound Hill, and had the delightful telephone number of Pound Hill 10!

102. *The Fox Hotel, Three Bridges (c1906).* The railway from London to Brighton was opened at Three Bridges in July 1841, and suddenly the village became important. People quickly realised that this mode of travel was cheaper, faster and more convenient than the traditional stagecoach, and with 4 trains in each direction every weekday, custom blossomed. The London and Brighton Railway Company, acting with commendable forethought, had already established a new hostelry close to the station, and the 1841 census records that the Fox Railway Inn (on the left) began life by housing 10 railway 'navvies' in that year. (The Fox was quickly sold into private hands in November 1843.) The railway bridge seen here incidentally is the original one, pulled down soon after this picture was taken in order to widen the line from two tracks to four, and replaced by the girder version familiar to modern commuters.

103. *Three Bridges Railway Station, looking north (c1903).* By 1843 a grand total of 11,000 passengers a week were using the Brighton line, and by 1844 those from the Crawley area could travel to London for only 2/- 3rd class (84 minutes), or 6/- 1st class (69 minutes). Three Bridges Station only had two platforms initially by the way (the two on the right, now platforms 4 and 5) and the original entrance at the top of Station Hill can just be glimpsed on the far right. A single track branch line was opened to Horsham in 1848, and another line, to East Grinstead, came into use in 1855. The latter was built by Georges Wythes from Reigate incidentally and its 7 miles cost £48,721. It ultimately closed on 1st January 1967, a victim of 'The Beeching axe'. In 1904, just after this photo was taken, the locomotive depot on the left was pushed eastwards and the station enlarged from two main lines to four, a new booking office and entrance hall being opened on the main road in 1911.

HAZELWICK MILL, THREE BRIDGES.

104. *Hazlewick watermill, Three Bridges (c1906).* Half a mile to the north of the railway station lay the picturesque form of Hazlewick watermill. Hazlewick is a name first recorded in the area in Saxon times and 'wick' or 'wic' was the Old English suffix denoting a farm (cf Gatwick), so Hazlewick may have initially been a farm surrounded by hazel coppice. The mill shown here, and used in its heyday for grinding flour, was probably of 18th century origin and, as you can see, was timber-framed and had a tiled roof, with a hoist facing onto the mill pond. (It may well have replaced an earlier building recorded as 'Hasticke Mill' in 1623.) The mill house nearby was of earlier date and, like Hazlewick Grange further up the lane, probably started life as a 17th century farmhouse. The mill was powered by the pond in front of it, and the flood gates controlling the water supply from the River Mole were sited close to the Fox Hotel and Three Bridges railway station.

105. *Three Bridges steam mill.* A survey carried out in Napoleonic times revealed that the watermill was only capable of turning out 1 sack of flour a day, compared to 16 at Ifield, so it can have been no surprise when Peter Caffyn, the miller of the day, decided to close the water-mill and resort to more modern methods in the 1890's. The new mill that he turned to was sited at the top of Station Hill, near the original entrance to Three Bridges station, and being steam driven was capable of much higher output than its predecessor. It wasn't as pretty as the old mill and its pond though, and even as a young child, in the 1940's, I remember my mother taking me along the lanes to visit what became one of the most popular local beauty spots. Decay gradually set in however, and the watermill was demolished in the 1950's in preparation for the new Hazlewick School. The steam mill eventually ground to a halt too – at the time of the Second World War – and now stands empty and forlorn minus its chimney.

106. *Worth, Crawley Lane (1906)*. Passing eastwards under the railway arch at Three Bridges Station (see 102), the traveller entered a small but ancient road leading to Pound Hill, and thence to the village of Worth. This road was known as Crawley Lane (now a backwater at the rear of a shopping parade), and in the days before the New Town contained two of the mere handful of thatched cottages remaining in the district. The one on the left was of 17th century origin, and actually consisted of two cottages, constructed chiefly of Sussex stone, with pretty casement windows. The one on the right was of later date, and in due course the thatch was replaced by tiles. Tom and Kate Dench ran a small shop here selling milk, dairy produce and meat, products no doubt of the Blackwater Farm owned by relatives just up the road. A pub called 'The Old Queen' existed just behind this cottage at one time, though it would seem to have ceased selling beer by the mid-19th century.

Worth Park, Sussex.

107. *Worth Park, Sussex (c1911)*. This red brick mansion was reached from a gatehouse on the northern side of Crawley Lane, and in Victorian times was owned by the Montefiore family. It was rebuilt in 1856, following a fire, and was the focal point for a huge estate stretching all the way to Crawley High Street. When Mrs. Montefiore died in 1915 the Crawley portion of the estate was sold, and five years later Worth Park itself changed hands for £30,000 guineas, becoming a school called Milton Mount College. This establishment, restricted to the daughters of Congregational Ministers, had come from Gravesend in Kent, where its former home had been requisitioned as a hospital for victims of venereal disease during the First World War. As the moral stigma of returning to such a home was unthinkable, the school moved to Worth, and enjoyed forty years here before amalgamating with a Bournemouth girls' school in 1962. The empty building was sold in 1967 and demolished soon afterwards.

108. *Worth School (1906)*. From Crawley Lane the road proceeded through Pound Hill and emerged at this crossroads, with Crabbet Park off to the left, Turners Hill ahead, and Worth Church School (as it originally was) on the right. It was built in 1852 and by 1909 could take 300 children, though the average attendance was stated as 196, testimony no doubt to the demands of farm work on the missing third! Worth in fact was always an exceedingly rural area, and despite having only a tiny village at its core, the parish covered an area of 8 miles by 5 and contained over 13,000 acres, the second largest parish in Sussex! William Cobbett stayed here several times on his 'Rural Rides' in the 1820's – at the home of a Mr. Brazier – and many other celebrities must have rattled through this sleepy rural parish in coaching days, since the Horley, Worth and Cuckfield stagecoach route was almost as important as the one through Crawley!

109. *Khyber Cottages, Worth.* Opposite the school, at the entrance to the same lane, stood a long L-shaped building, the southern part of which was the parish workhouse in days of yore. (Seen at far left.) It dated from the late 1700's and was recorded as having 55 inmates in 1852, but as mention of it ceases in 1866 its life must have been fairly short – perhaps a hundred years at the most. The first window that you can see on the left marked the warden's quarters incidentally. By the time that this photo was taken, probably in the 1910's, the building had been converted into cottages, with a grocer's shop on the end which also functioned as a sweetshop and tea rooms. The proprietor, Edwin Rapley, can be seen standing at the gate. The whole building was demolished by the New Town Commission in the 1950's. (Crawley also had its workhouse, on the northern side of the village, and latterly called 'Yew Tree Cottage'.)

110. *Street House, Worth (1906).* The lane running south between workhouse and school used to be the main road in coaching days, and is still guarded by a former toll cottage. Street House, just round the corner, dates from the 17th century, and has a Horsham stone roof and a 14th century cellar. It began life as an inn, but lost its custom when the railway swept through from Surrey. Worth was originally *in* Surrey of course, and is recorded in the Domesday Book as 'Orde' under the entry for Reigate hundred. It belonged to Oswol in the reign of Edward the Confessor (1042-1066), and at the time of the survey (1086) was assessed as having only 1 villein and 4 oxen on less than 90 acres of taxable land. After passing through many hands the manor was sold to ironmaster Leonard Gale in 1698, and for a brief period, from 1707 to 1762, was in the same ownership as the Manor of Crawley. From then on it came into the hands of the Blunt family, whose descendants still live in the area.

111. *Worth Church.* Ethelred the Unready or King Canute were probably on the throne when Christianity crept out of the giant forests of the Weald and arrived at Worth in the early 11th century. This church is quite the oldest and most famous building in the Crawley area and experts agree that it was built in Saxon times – even though the Normans who compiled the Domesday Book somehow overlooked it! Saxon features still in evidence are the massive 22ft high chancel arch, the vertical stone strips decorating the exterior, and three of the original divided windows (two in mid-photo), from which arrows could be fired when the church was needed as a refuge against Danish attackers. There is also a curious 'Knight's Door', a particularly high one, which it is said permitted the entrance of a man on horseback to spend the night in vigil before being knighted! The tower seen here was only added in 1871 when the church was restored, and replaced a much prettier, wooden, shingled one over the north portico.

112. *Wood sawing, Tilgate Forest (c1907)*. The forest surrounding Worth and its historic church was part of the gigantic forest of Andreas-weald, which swept across the northern swathes of Sussex in the centuries before the Norman Conquest. In medieval times the 'Forest of Worth' covered the parishes of Worth, Crawley, Ardingly, Slaugham and Balcombe, and formed part of the possessions of the Warennes in the Rape of Lewes. In the 15th and 16th centuries though it began to be divided, and the section south of Crawley came to be known as the Forest of Tilgate. My own associations with Crawley stem from Tilgate Forest in fact, for my father, a timber merchant, came from Epsom to run a sawmill here in 1939, and became a Crawley resident for the rest of his life. In 1963, however, he established his own tiny sawmill at Haywards Heath, and surprisingly enough, the equipment that he used was not so very different to that shown here in the early years of the century.

113. *Tilgate Brickyard, Crawley, Sussex (c1908)*. Tucked away on the fringes of the forest, a mile and a half south of Crawley, lay Tilgate Brickyard. This had been established in Victorian times and the pond in the foreground was the result of clay digging, an iron stake in mid-forest bearing witness to the time when a horse would be driven round and round, churning the clay to the required consistency after excavation. By 1910 at the latest brickmaking had ceased however, and the buildings seen here were being used as a sawmill and grinding mill for the Tilgate estate. Indeed, not only was all the corn required for feeding the estate's animal population prepared here, but, up until the First World War, tubs were inserted in the pond for sheep washing as well. When the Tilgate Estate was sold in 1939, E. Longhurst & Sons, a firm of Epsom timber merchants, opened a branch sawmill here, and this in turn was taken over by Tilgate Pallets in 1957, the sawmilling side of operations ceasing in 1963.

114. *Tilgate Mansion (c1909).* 'Amongst those which attract the attention... are Tilgate House and Tilgate Manor... which from their contiguity to the forest, the elegance of the mansions, extent of well and carefully arranged grounds, aided by a noble and expansive lake, present a scene of almost unsurpassing beauty.' Thus wrote the author of a local directory in 1866, shortly after John Nix (a member of a London banking family) purchased the estate and had this imposing mansion – Tilgate House – specially constructed for himself. Tilgate Manor, the other house referred to, seems to have been situated near the bay of the main lake, and was possibly the original 'Manor House', the manor having first been recorded in 1647 and described as 'a messuage and farm called Tillgate' when sold in 1676. A 'messuage' was a house built before living memory! The Manor House is described as 'unoccupied' by 1878 and is no longer mentioned by 1895.

115. *Tilgate Mansion, Interior (c1906).* The message on this card reads: 'Dear Kit, I don't think you have got one of these have you? It is the saloon of the little place I am spending my honeymoon.' 'Little place' was certainly tongue in cheek as, apart from this huge hallway flanked by marble pillars, it also contained a billiards room, study, three living rooms and eight bedrooms! In its heyday it was accompanied by a small army of servants and estate workers too, for not only the house but also a little matter of 2,000 acres required upkeep! Why, the estate even had its own gamekeeper and shepherd! Costs mounted and the number of employees dwindled however, and in 1939 the entire estate was put up for auction – in 74 lots. (One of the purchasers being Sir Malcolm Campbell, who acquired the lakes for boat trials.) – By 1964, when ownership of both mansion and lakes had passed to Crawley Council, the house was beyond repair and was demolished, though the lakes now form the heart of the aptly named Tilgate Park.

116. *Plough Cottage, Ifield (1905)*. Ifield lies just over a mile north-west of Crawley and, 1,000 years ago, was recorded as having 9 families, 6 acres of meadowland, 6 pigs and 1 plough. St. Margaret's Church, seen in the background, probably dates from the 12th century and contains fine 14th century sculptures of Sir John de Ifelde and his wife Margaret. A settlement gradually began to develop around the Green from the 15th century onwards, but it was only in Elizabethan times that Plough Cottage (seen on the right) came into existence. Complete with an attractive 'minstrel's gallery' it became home for the Old Plough Inn from c1833 to c1910, when it moved into converted stables next door. Sir John Shurley was probably Lord of the Manor when the cottage was first built incidentally, the Manor of Ifield having passed from Alwi in 1066 through the families of Poynings, Covert, Holles and Rodney amongst others, before expiring with Sir John Drughorn in 1943.

117. *Ifield Forge (c1877)*. A few yards to the east of the Old Plough Inn was the blacksmith's forge run by the King family. A smithy is recorded close to Ifield Green as far back as 1761, but it was probably the predecessor to the one pictured here as the tithe map of 1841 shows the blacksmith's on the opposite side of the road. Believe it or not this building seems to have been a shop, run by Elizabeth Burberry, at the start of Victoria's reign, and was converted to a smithy either when John King was in charge (1846), or after Michael King became owner (about 1852). As you can see it appears to have been built with whatever materials were to hand at the time, the walls being partly brick and partly timber slabs from the outside of the tree, with a weather-boarded gable at this end and the sophistication of a tiled roof! – In later life the motor car brought a decline in the blacksmith's trade, the building fell into disuse and it eventually became part of the cottage next door.

118. *Ifield Watermill (c1913).* This elegant, weather-boarded cornmill stands on the site of Ifield's original 'Forge', which was in use by 1574, and burnt to the ground by Puritan troops during the Civil War. The man-made 'hammer pond' which survived it was joined by a cornmill in 1683, and after ownership by Thomas Middleton, the Quaker Garton family, ironmaster Leonard Gale and London merchant Abraham Golsmid, the building came into the hands of Thomas Durrant early in the 19th century. Either during or shortly before his ownership it was rebuilt, and it is probably the new mill that was noted as producing a magnificent output of 16 sacks of flour per day in Napoleonic times. The installation of a steam engine in 1835 helped to stave off fierce competition from other 19th century mills, including a windmill on Ifield Green, but changing times and labour shortages in the First World War resulted in closure around 1927. The mill has recently been restored.

119. *The Village Stores, Ifield (1920's)*. Francis Collins' shop was sited to the north-east of Ifield Green, and this delightful picture shows the entire 'staff' posing outside their emporium. The adverts for Sunlight Soap, a 'Guarantee of Purity', and American Lamp Oil speak vividly of another era! The earliest shop recorded in Ifield was in 1711, bordering the churchyard, and there was a trio of shops to the south-west of the village green by 1833 – a butcher's, shoemaker's and wheelwright's – but isolated ventures such as that run by Mr. Collins were somehow more representative of a scattered rural community. Indeed it is a curious fact that Ifield, though in existence for over a thousand years, has never possessed a conventional 'village high street' – a feature it shares with Worth, its Domesday contemporary, and a marked contrast to the later communities of Crawley, Handcross and Three Bridges!

The Mill, Lowfield Heath.

120. *The Mill, Lowfield Heath (c1906)*. By virtue of its position just off the London-Brighton Road the windmill at Lowfield Heath was probably the most widely known in the Crawley area. It first appeared on a map in 1762, and this was the year in which, according to unsubstantiated local tradition, it was moved from its original home on Hookwood common, some 2 miles to the north. In 1827 it made legal history when Mr. Parker, the tenant miller, unsuccesssfully applied for an injunction preventing the enclosure of Lowfield Heath, on the grounds that the accompanying enlargement of Lovel House literally 'took the wind out of his sails'! Around 1880 the sails ceased to revolve, and though a portable steam engine prolonged the activity of this attractive post mill for a few more years, it ceased working altogether c1895. Dummy sails were fitted and restorarion was attempted in the 1930's and again in the 1960's, but recent deterioration has been formed to effect a rescue – removal to Gatwick Zoo and accompanying renovation being scheduled for 1987.

121. *Lowfield Heath (Church Road).* Balancing on the border between Surrey and Sussex, Lowfield Heath was a small, dusty hamlet 2 miles north of Crawley. It probably got its name from a man called 'Lowe' recorded there in 1332, though the 'Lowfeild Heath' of 1662 was corrupted to the yokel version of 'Lovel Heath' in the 18th century. As the later name implied, the straggling village farmhouses were at one time spread around an area of 'common land' or heath. The land surrounding the windmill was enclosed in 1827 however, and it is likely that the remainder was enclosed in 1846. Though several attractive timber-framed buildings survived into the present century, the architectural highlight was the church, St. Michael's, constructed of yellow sandstone in 1867 (on right of picture), and designed by eminent Victorian William Burges. It suffered a humiliation in 1897 when the dedication of the new organ had to be abandoned as local roads were under 4 feet of water!

122. *Lowfield Heath, The village Shop (c1906).* Despite the fact that the village had been part of the parish of Charlwood since Norman times, and was conveniently situated on the Brighton Road, it never grew to any substantial size. At the turn of the century, its centre consisted only of a school, public house, blacksmith's, wheelwright's, church – and this building, the village shop, which also doubled as a post office. The arrival of Gatwick Aerodrome in 1930 had little effect on the small hamlet, but when the new airport was built and opened in 1958 it was a different story. Houses on the northern and western sides of the village were demolished to make way for the main runway, others fell into dereliction, some were taken over and removed by property developers. Though the village struggled gamely on till the early 1970's it was a hopeless battle – and today only the church survives as a reminder of a once proud community.

123. *Gatwick Racecourse.* Sporting hooliganism is considered to be a modern phenomenon, but public behaviour at Croydon racecourses became so bad during the 1880's that Queen Victoria banned all further race meetings from taking place in London. As Gatwick was considered suitably far from the Queen's wrath it was decided to construct a new course here, and in 1890 land was acquired and work commenced. The name Gatwick means 'goat farm' incidentally – and the purchase included part of the original 'Manor of Gatwick' granted to John de Gatwick and his heirs by King Henry III in the 13th century. The new racecourse, complete with its own railway station, opened in 1891, and for the next fifty years an average of 16 days racing took place every year. After 1940 use was spasmodic and the final meeting took place on 28th April 1948. The course now lies buried under Gatwick Airport, though its bandstand still survives, in Queen's Square, Crawley.

124. *Gatwick Aerodrome (c1930).* On 1st August 1930, a pilot named Ronald Walters opened a new aerodrome on 105 acres of land at Hunts Green, just south of Gatwick Racecourse. Three years later the business changed hands for £13,500 – and the new owner, Maurice Jackaman, was a 29 year old aviation enthusiast with only two years flying experience! The Air Ministry now became involved in developing Gatwick as an emergency airfield and work began on a new terminal building in 1935. The official opening of the new airport took place on Saturday 6th June 1936 and was attended by Sir Malcolm and Lady Campbell together with Amy Mollison (née Johnson). A new company, British Airways Ltd., was already operating passenger flights to Paris (£4.5/- single, £ 6.0.0 return) and mail flights to Scandinavia. Edward G. Robinson and Ralph Richardson filmed 'Thunder in the City' there in 1937, and a huge flying display in June 1938 attracted 150,000 people. Gatwick was 'off the ground'!